THE BEATLES CONQUER AMERICA

Other Avon Books
on the Beatles

THE BEATLES: THE LONG AND WINDING ROAD
A History of the Beatles on Record
by Neville Stannard

THE BEATLES: WORKING CLASS HEROES
The History of the Beatles' Solo Recordings
by Neville Stannard & John Tobler

THE BEATLES: PAPERBACK WRITERS
The History of the Beatles in Print
by Bill Harry

Coming Soon
THE BEATLES: BEATLEMANIA
The History of the Beatles on Film
by Bill Harry

Avon Books are available at special quantity discounts for bulk purchases for sales promotions, premiums, fund raising or educational use. Special books, or book excerpts, can also be created to fit specific needs.

For details write or telephone the office of the Director of Special Markets, Avon Books, Dept. FP, 1790 Broadway, New York, New York 10019, 212-399-1357. *IN CANADA:* Director of Special Sales, Avon Books of Canada, Suite 210, 2061 McCowan Rd., Scarborough, Ontario M1S 3Y6, 416-293-9404.

THE BEATLES CONQUER AMERICA

The Photographic Record of Their First American Tour

DEZO HOFFMANN

AVON
PUBLISHERS OF BARD, CAMELOT, DISCUS AND FLARE BOOKS

The photographs in this book were all taken between January 14 and February 22, 1964 when I travelled with the Beatles from London to New York, Washington D.C., Miami, and back to London, on their first American tour. The tour was preceded by three weeks of dates in Paris, which are also included here. Even though the boys had won the French over quite easily and were becoming more confident, none of us could imagine the phenomenal success they were about to find in the States. The day before the boys flew to New York, Paul said quite innocently, "They've got everything over there. What do they want *us* for?"

I was working as a press photographer specialising in show-business personalities when I first met the Beatles in 1962. Although I had already had an exciting and eventful life travelling around as a war correspondent in the Spanish Civil War, joining the Czech army in World War II, and working as house photographer at the London Palladium, when I came across the Beatles, I was completely captivated by them. They were so unlike the typical celebrities I was used to dealing with. They had undeniable star quality, yet were so unspoilt. They were so much fun to be with; totally spontaneous, charming, full of playful wit and youthful energy.

As I got to know the boys better, I felt I must help to create a totally unique visual image for them. I didn't want to use the same angles or techniques as other photographers; conventional posed shots wouldn't do for the Beatles. I tried to put them in stimulating situations and locales that would bring out their marvellous personalities. I wanted to present them in a way that would allow them to just be themselves. As an artist, I couldn't be satisfied until I had somehow captured their magic on film.

People often ask me how I was lucky enough to be invited along with the Beatles on this tour; in fact, I didn't have to be invited. In those days I was one of the family, and it was assumed that I would go everywhere the boys went. People also ask me why I was allowed to get so close to them. I like to think we had such a good personal relationship not so much because they respected my work as a photographer, but because they trusted me as a person. I think they knew that I was only there because I was genuinely swept off my feet. I certainly wasn't there to make money out of them; money never came into it. I had to sort out a sponsorship and secure advances from various newspapers and magazines to pay my way. In fact, along with the Beatles, I lost out heavily on the merchandising deals, all of which made great use of my pictures. The truth is, I fell for the Beatles the way millions of fans have done since.

Sometimes my adventures with the Beatles in those early days seem like some amazing once-upon-a-time fairy tale, and I wonder if it all really happened. Fortunately, when the Beatles and I inevitably moved away from each other's orbit, I was left with a legacy of photographs and film. One of my most precious keepsakes is a short zany colour movie of the boys and I together, taken by the Beatles themselves in 1963.

I'm thankful for the chance I was given to photograph them at their happy-go-lucky best and for the chance to share my memories with you.

To all lovers of the Beatles' music throughout the world

AVON BOOKS
A division of
The Hearst Corporation
1790 Broadway
New York, New York 10019

Copyright © 1984 by Dezo Hoffmann
Published by arrangement with Virgin Books, Ltd.
Library of Congress Catalog Card Number: 84-045883
ISBN: 0-380-89805-5

All rights reserved, which includes the right to reproduce this book or portions thereof in any form whatsoever except as provided by the U.S. Copyright Law. For information address Frommer-Price Literary Agency, 185 East 85th Street, New York, New York 10028.

First Avon Printing, August 1985

AVON TRADEMARK REG. U.S. PAT. OFF. AND IN OTHER COUNTRIES, MARCA REGISTRADA, HECHO EN U.S.A.

Printed in the U.S.A.

DON 10 9 8 7 6 5 4 3 2 1

CONTENTS

PARIS 10

NEW YORK 30

WASHINGTON DC 78

MIAMI 102

RETURN TO LONDON 154

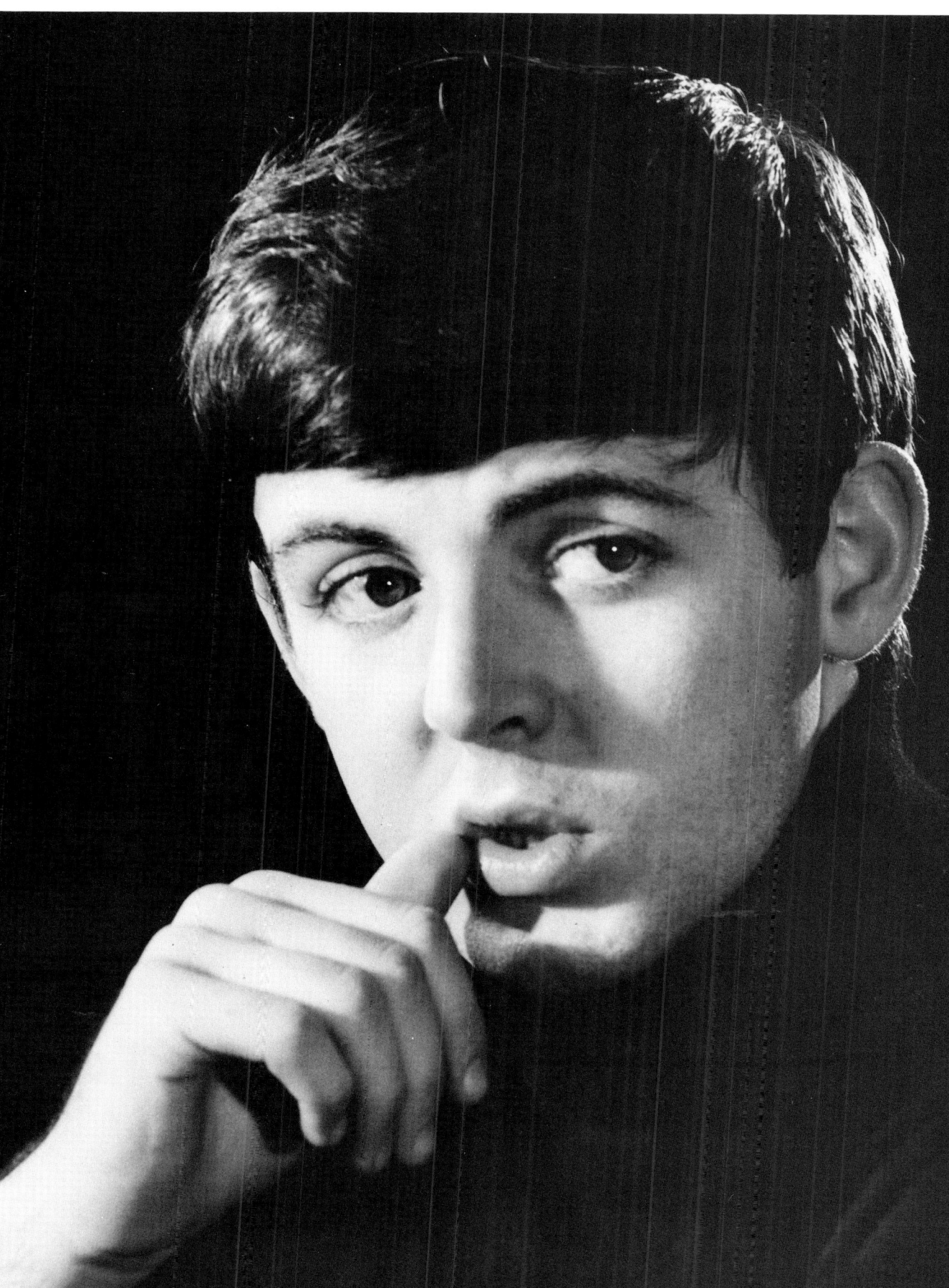

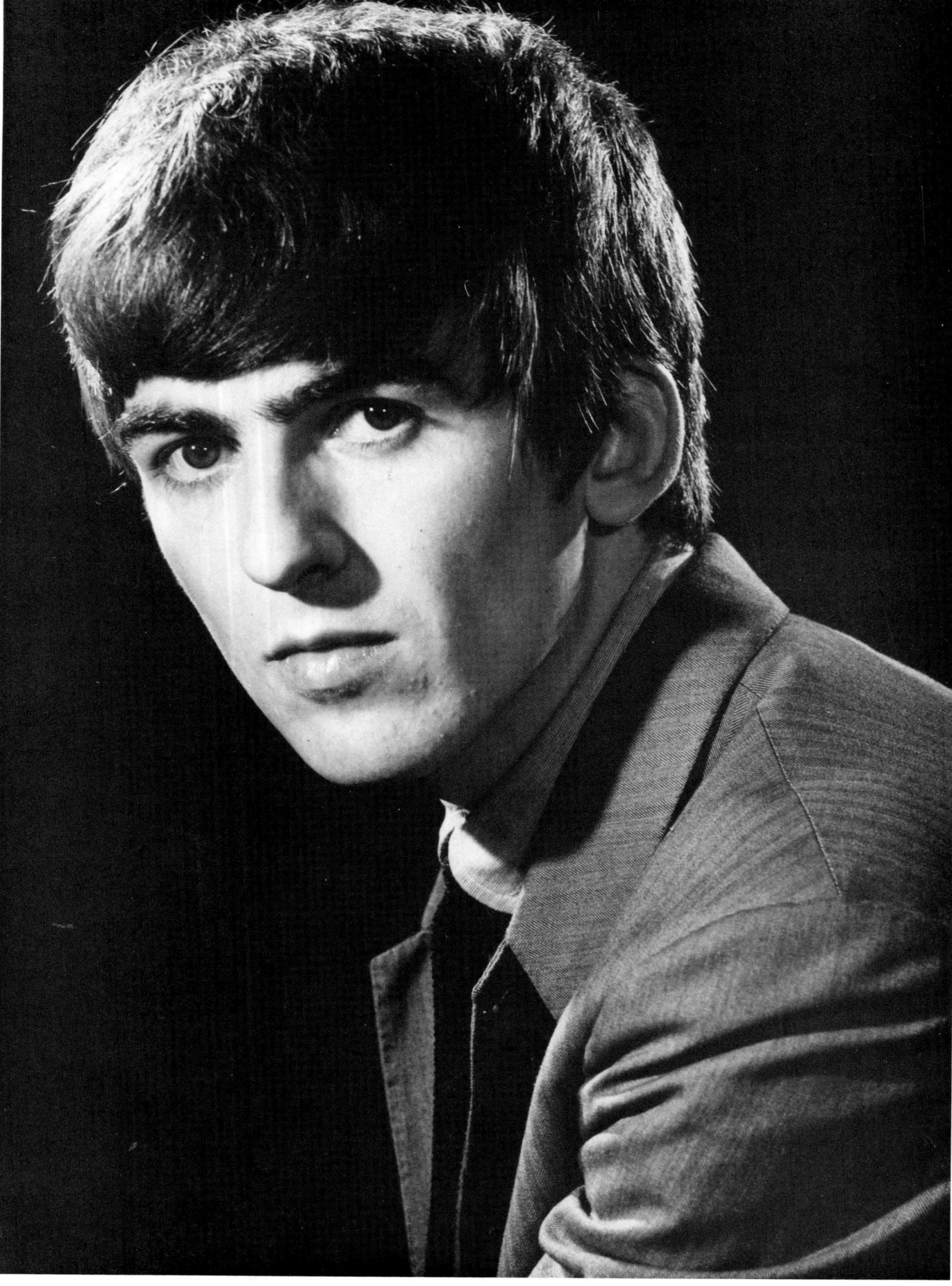

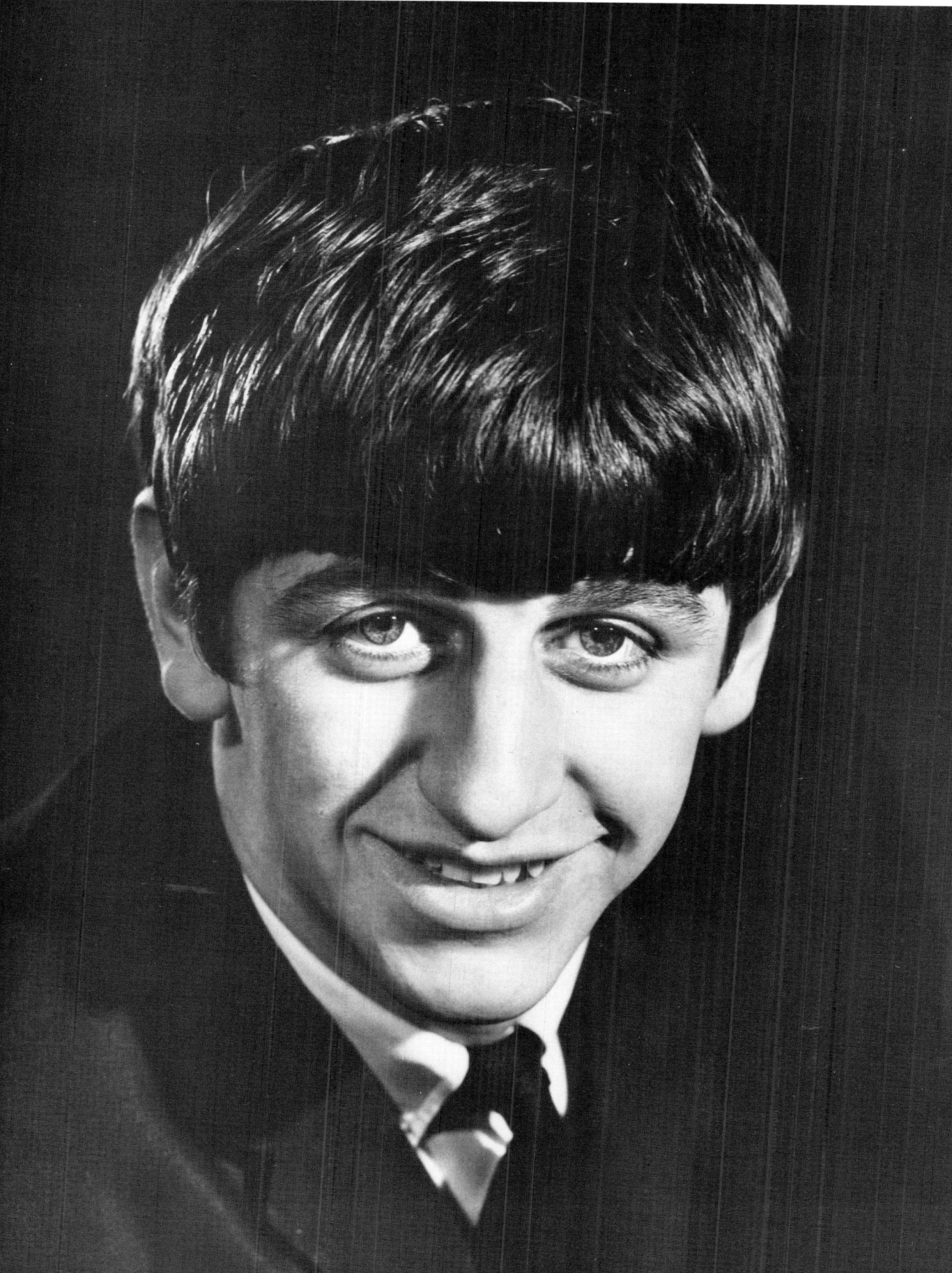

PARIS

I flew to Le Bourget airport on January 14th, 1964 with John, Paul and George. Ringo was fogbound in Liverpool and came a day late, missing a massive send-off at Heathrow.

The Beatles' manager, Brian Epstein, had booked the entire entourage into the George V, one of Europe's finest hotels, and when the boys saw it they gasped at its magnificence. Here they had their first taste of many new things, including a new gastronomical delight. Their waiter was appalled at the Beatle diet, – rather working-class English, – of bacon, eggs, and beans, and persuaded them to try crepes suzettes. They began experimenting with fillings, and were soon living on crepes of every description.

On their second day in Paris, the Beatles were interviewed by the political commentator from the American corporation, Westinghouse. The man from Westinghouse hadn't heard their music, and didn't even know there were four of them. Nevertheless the boys conducted themselves very wittily. The tape was sent back to the US where it was edited and broadcast nationally. When the Beatles heard the interview later in the States, they maintained it was one of the best they'd ever given.

The first French concert was at the Cyrano Theatre in Versailles. Onstage the Beatles were tired and nervous after a day of interviews, and unfortunately a lot of newspapermen turned up to cover the concert. Apart from the press, the audience was mostly local townsfolk, so the small crowd was rather sedate. The reviews the next day reflected the lukewarm response.

The Beatles were always very accommodating photographically. They always did all I asked, so I decided to try some Parisian-flavoured shots. Our January visit was cold, dull and misty, but I thought it best to get some pictures of the boys while it was still safe to do so. Although the boys were a bit fed up because they didn't seem to be instantly winning over the French, I knew instinctively that it would only be a matter of time. I figured they'd need about a week to get Paris talking; in fact, the fans were beginning to flock around them by the third day.

George stayed at the hotel most of the time. He wasn't feeling well and had a bit of work to do, as he'd agreed to write a column for the *Daily Express* while in Paris. This was made easier by the presence of Derek Taylor, who virtually ghosted the article for him. The two struck up a friendship and Taylor later became the Beatles' press officer.

I set off with the other three, taking them on a little tour of the city. We bought postcards on the Champs Elysses, wandered around quaint backstreets, drank coffee at little pavement cafes, and explored the Left Bank. Here the boys' spirits were immediately lifted when they met the avant-garde painters who had not only heard of the Beatles, but had been busy painting vivid caricatures of them! The sight of themselves on canvas revived their flagging spirits.

The main reason for the trip to Paris was a three-week season at the Olympia, a music-hall theatre. Advance ticket sales were really made on the strength of the better known artists on the bill, – Sylvie Vartan and Trini Lopez, but the audience was polite to the new act. The audience was mostly male, and they were seriously interested in the Beatles' music. They kept quiet during the performance, applauding only after a particularly good solo, saving their appreciation until the end of each song. It was a real pleasure to actually *hear* the Beatles perform.

On the first night someone kicked a wire onstage and the whole house shorted. The lights went out and there was no amplification. Just as the catcalls started, Ringo saved the day. He suddenly became a Gene Krupa on his kit, pounding away like crazy. Everyone went wild, chanting "Rin-Go! Rin-Go!" After that the Paris boys began to identify with him, dressing like him and wearing Beatle wigs. Ringo was really the most popular Beatle in France, possibly because he was the most French-looking of the boys. This was a nice boost for Ringo, as at this time he wasn't quite a full-fledged member of the Beatles. He wasn't officially in the group until after the American tour, although Brian Epstein told him "You're in" after the success of the Paris shows.

It wasn't until *Paris Match*, the European equivalent of *Life* magazine, did a colour front-page and inside spread on the Beatles that the tide began to turn in their favour, and the article almost didn't happen. The magazine phoned PR Brian Sommerville one morning telling him a photographer and an English-speaking reporter were on their way. They had 90 minutes before the deadline for the next week's issue. It was nine o'clock in the morning and the boys had gone to bed only two hours earlier, after spending all night composing. Sommerville was scared to wake them and came to my room to ask me if I'd do it. I walked into their rooms and started to shake them, telling them how important this job was for them. Suddenly, John's face appeared from under the sheets, asking quite innocently, "Is *Paris Match* more important than the *Musical Express?*"

I persuaded them to let *Paris Match* do the session right there and then in the suite, photographing them washing and shaving, getting ready for the day ahead. The session turned out beautifully.

On the third day I was sitting in a restaurant near the George V when the Beatles' road manager Mal Evans rushed in, saying that Brian Epstein wanted to see me urgently. Back at the hotel Epstein was bursting to tell me the news: 'I Want To Hold Your Hand' had hit number one in the *Cashbox* American Hot 100.

The Beatles themselves were completely dumbfounded. They simply couldn't speak, – not even John. They sat like kittens at Brian's feet. I broke the silence and told them this was surely an open invitation to visit the States, and that now they would be a must for the Ed Sullivan Show. Epstein had already done some negotiating with Sullivan a few months earlier.

After ten days in France I had to return to London. Today no-one mentions the French tour, – not even the so-called historians, but although we didn't know it at the time, it was an invaluable rehearsal. I'm still convinced that staying at the George V, playing at the Olympia and meeting the world's press, gave the Beatles the self-confidence that enabled them to handle America so well a month later.

PAGE 12
When the Beatles passed through customs at Le Bourget, I explained to them that the French are very particular about the way they salute, – the forefinger should be touching the temple. "If you salute this way," I said, "it will make you very popular in France."

PAGE 13
A limousine from London arrives for the boys' personal use. They graciously posed with car and chauffeur for me and for posterity, outside the Hotel George V.

PAGE 14
Some of the busy eating sessions with the new addiction, crepes suzettes. In the foreground is the chef's portable spirit cooker. Eventually the waiter had to move his portable frying pan and spirit cooker into their suite!

PAGE 15
Top: Unfortunately I don't have the name of this gentleman from the French office of the Westinghouse Corporation; I hope he will forgive me. He was so doubled up with laughter during the interview that he could hardly question them. He couldn't memorise who was who, so he wrote down their names from left to right. When the Beatles noticed this, they started changing places to confuse him even more. Bottom: France's major pop radio programme Europe Number One tried very hard to get them to sing 'I Want To Hold Your Hand' in French, but the boys were not particularly gifted at languages. However, they did a fabulous interview in English, which was simultaneously translated.

PAGE 16
As we climbed up to Sacre Coeur in Montemartre we entered a small square with artists displaying their paintings, most of which depicted Paris street scenes. Nobody was taking any notice of the Beatles, but as we approached the middle of the square there was a yell of delight from John. He'd spotted a painting of the Beatles, a sort of surrealistic caricature. Everyone forgot the freezing cold and gathered around John to admire the six-foot long canvas and pose happily with the painter, a White Russian, who was thrilled to meet them in the flesh.

PAGE 17
Top & Bottom left: Buying postcards in the Champs Elysses for friends and relatives at home. Small crowds gathered, but it was the photographers who aroused their curiosity, rather than the Beatles. The French public didn't really know yet who the Beatles were Top right: A very cold day. We went into a bistro for a hot cup of tea. Instead we got a cup of good French coffee from the young lady behind the counter. She was so attractive I asked her to pose outside on the pavement with the Beatles. She'd never heard of them, but did me the favour and went upstairs to change into some flimsy French postcard-style clothes. It only took me three minutes to get the pictures, but she was blue with cold, despite John snuggling up against her at the back. Bottom right: On the Champs Elysses we went into a Citroën showroom and asked the manager for permission to pose with a vintage car. "With pleasure," he said, adding the proviso that they didn't sit on it in case it collapsed. The boys did completely the opposite and sat inside posing by the showroom window like dummies at Madame Tussauds. Outside on the street nobody even stopped and looked. Eventually, this picture was used as a press handout by NEMS.

PAGE 18
This was taken not far from the Eiffel Tower. I was attracted mainly by the graffiti.

PAGE 19
This doorway was actually a brilliant blue and would have made a beautiful colour sleeve picture. It also gave me a premonition of visiting America, the home of Ford.

PAGE 20
Top: The facade of the Olympia in daylight showing the names of the artists featured for the three-week season. Bottom: I thought it would be rather nice to immortalise this poster made by the Olympia because they used Astrid Kirschner's photographs. I believe these are some of the most impressive and tasteful pictures of the Beatles from this particular period. I tried to take all my pictures in the same clean-cut style. Astrid, along with Klaus Voorman, befriended the Beatles in Hamburg, but she didn't care for the 'Hamburg look' photos and always photographed the boys against plain backgrounds and in nice clothes. It was Astrid who first suggested the boys grow their hair long.

PAGE 21
Top: En route to rehearsals at the Olympia in the English limousine. Bottom: The first signs of the Parisian youth showing their appreciation of the Beatles. This shot was taken in the narrow back street where the Olympia stage door came out.

PAGE 22
Top left: Before the show I had the opportunity to take pictures of the crowds going into the Olympia concert hall. Notice the predominace of male ticket holders. Of course this may have been due to Sylvia Vartan. Top right: Onstage at the Olympia, when the lights came on after the blackout. Centre: In the foyer bar of the Olympia before the show – a refreshing break with the Fab Four. They were quite pleased with themselves at finding a place to hide for a few minutes. Bottom left: The stars of the show backstage in the Beatles' dressing room at the Olympia. Although the boys don't look particularly happy, they really enjoyed the company of Trini Lopez and Sylvie.

PAGE 23
In a Parisian photographic studio: the Beatles minus George posing a la Française.

PAGE 24
Top: The memorable night when the elegram arrived saying 'I Want To Hold Your Hand' was number one in Cashbox. The Beatles celebrated not with champagne but with their usual – milk and cokes. They were somewhat exhausted making plans, – they knew this was the big turning point in their career. Bottom: Here I am encouraging them to consider touring America.

PAGE 25
The hotel didn't have a big enough stars-and-stripes so I went to the US Embassy and borrowed this one. America here we come!

PAGES 26 & 27
These were taken during the session with Paris Match, after I suggested they interview and photograph the Beatles just getting up in the morning.

PAGE 28
John with a copy of Cashbox, the American publication which first showed I Want To Hold Your Hand at number one. This was also a proud moment for George Martin; it was his persistence that got Capitol to finally release a Beatles record.

PAGE 29
Back in London outside the National Portrait Gallery, I spotted a pavement artist who was portraying from memory the late John F. Kennedy. This portrait was surrounded by the four Beatles, and by a strange coincidence John Lennon was next to President Kennedy. Shortly after I took this picture, torrential rain washed away the work of the unknown artist.

PARIS

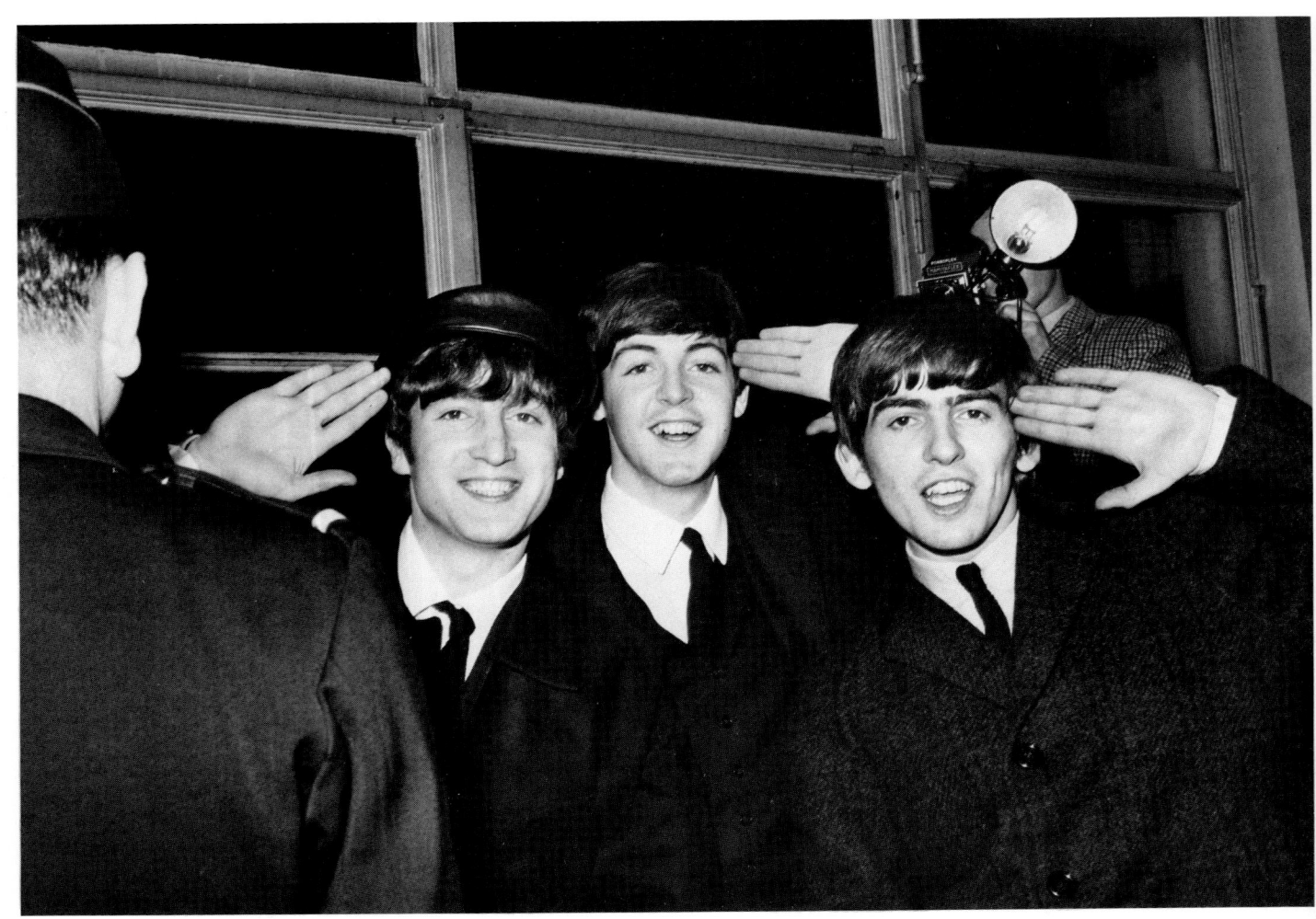

PARIS

PARIS

PARIS

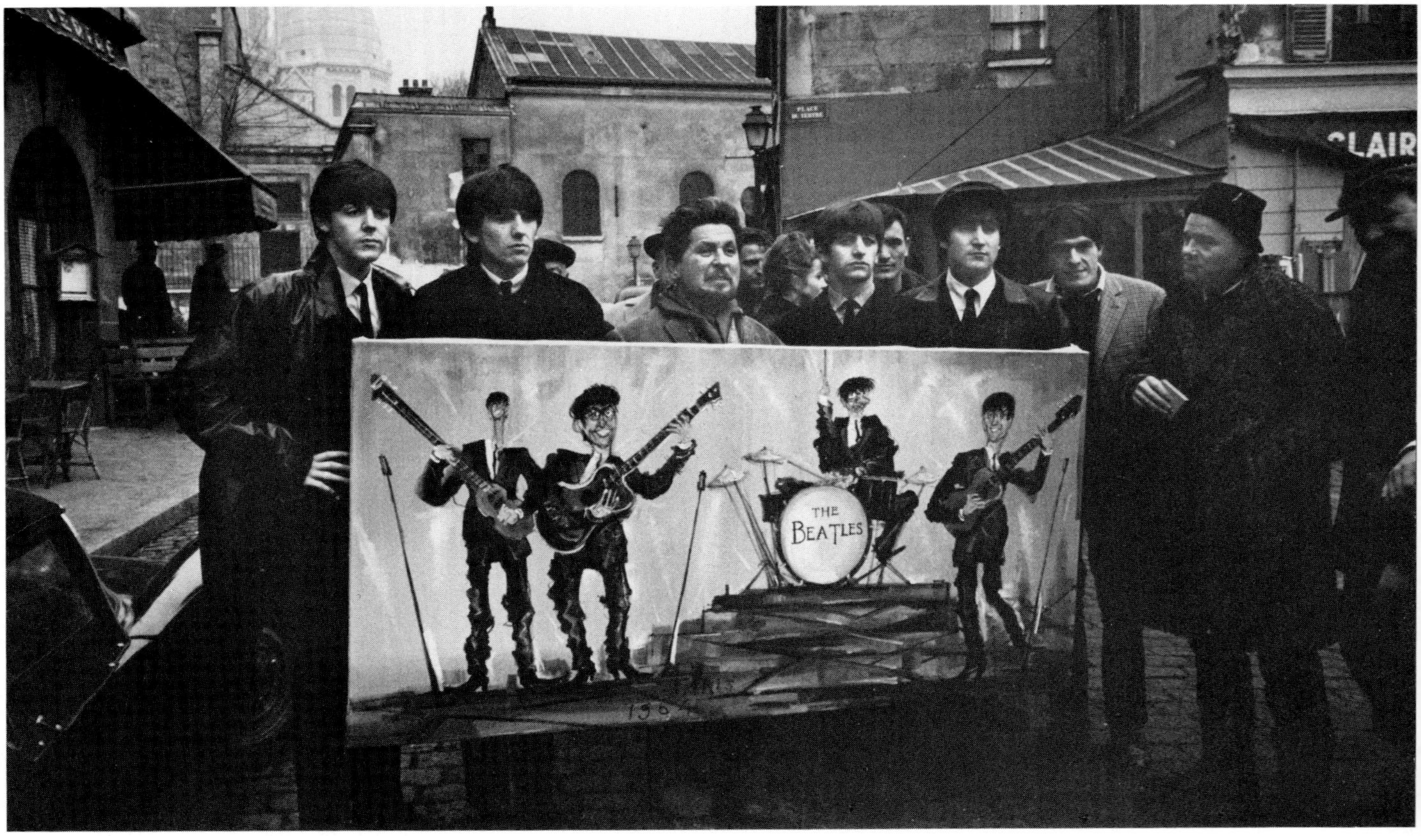
THE
BEATLES

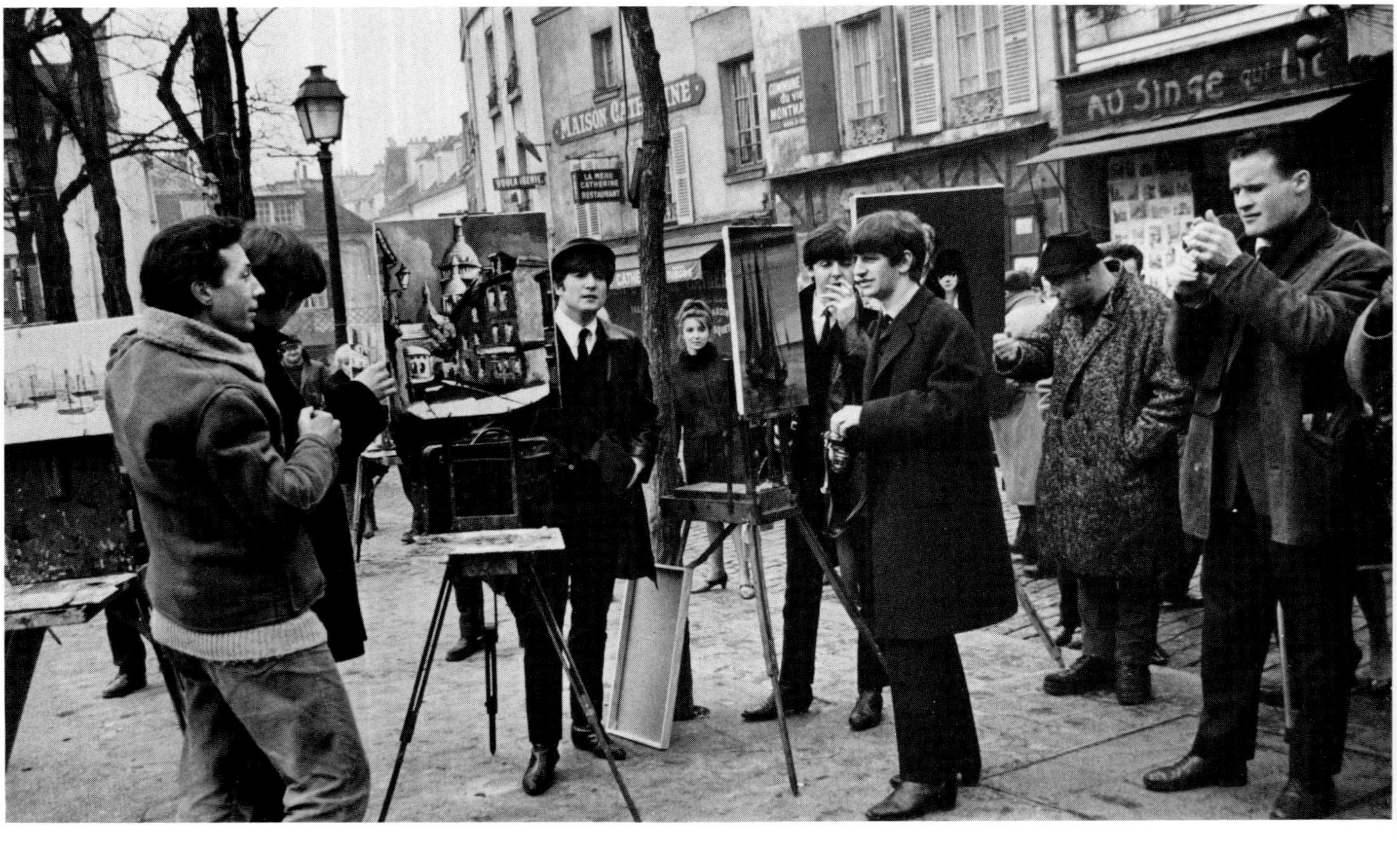
AU SINGE QUI LIT
MAISON CATHERINE
LA MERE CATHERINE RESTAURANT

PARIS

PARIS

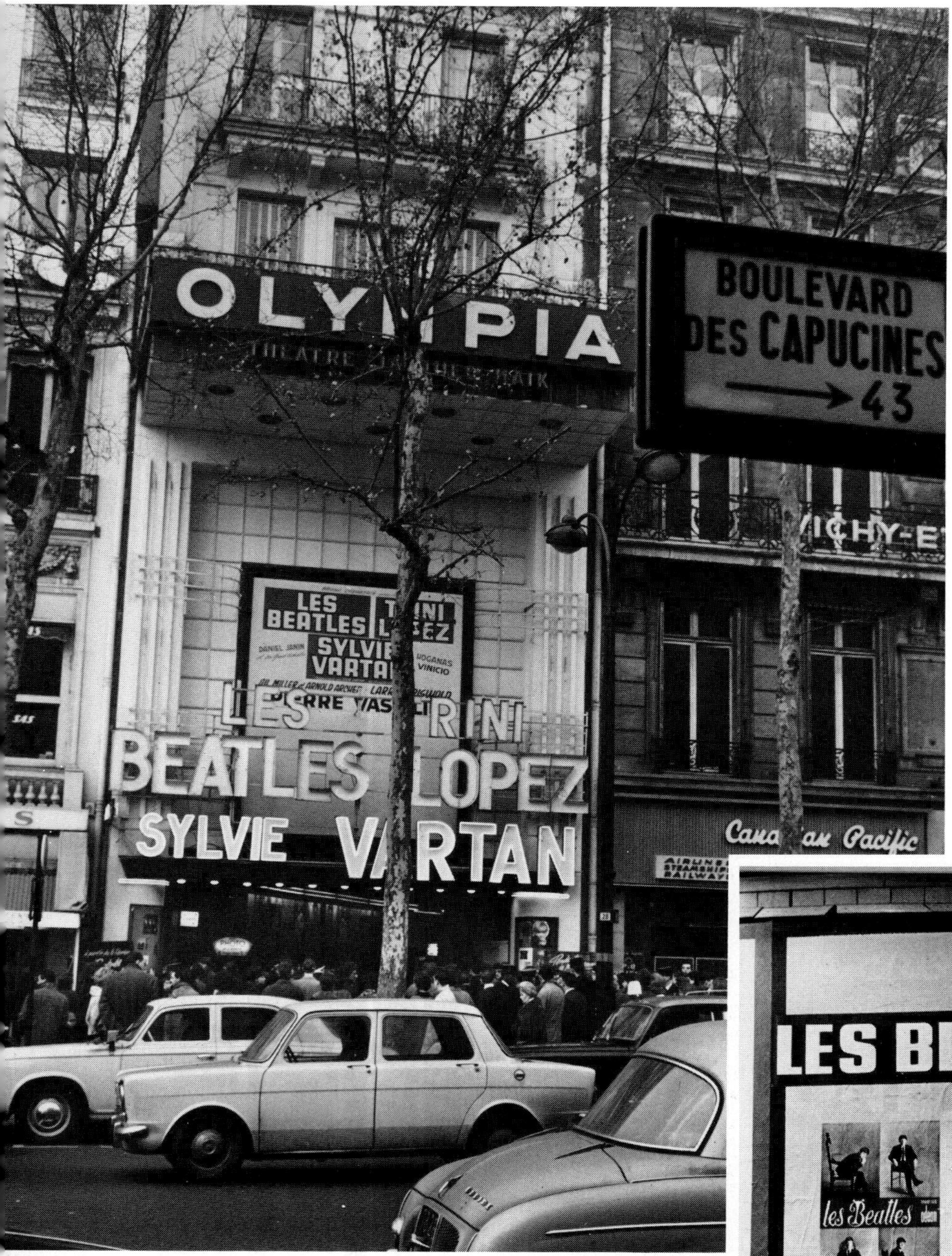
OLYMPIA
BOULEVARD
DES CAPUCINES
43
LES BEATLES
SYLVIE VARTAN
LES BEATLES
TRINI LOPEZ
SYLVIE VARTAN
Canadian Pacific

LES BEATLES - disques odeon
les Beatles odeon
LES BEATLES à l'OLYMPIA
DU 16 JANVIER
AU 4 FEVRIER

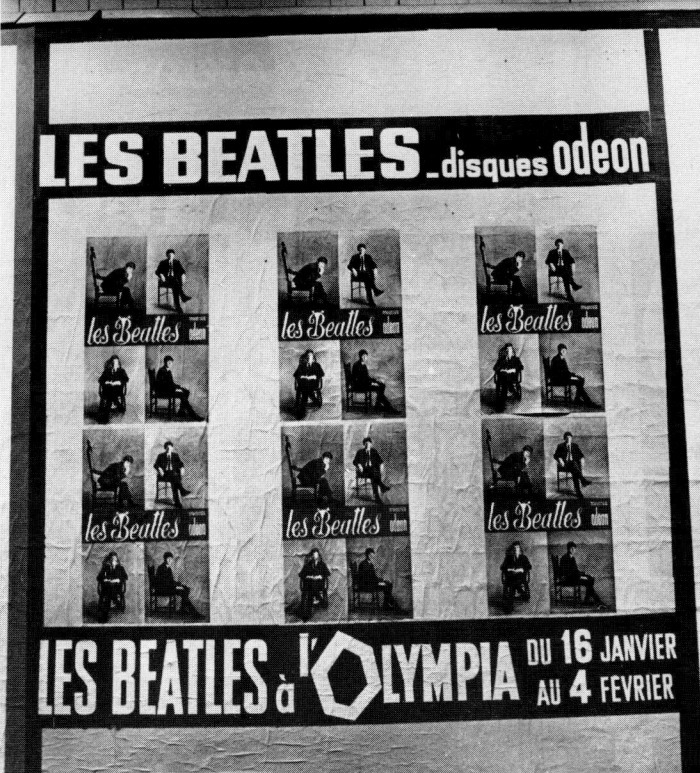

PARIS

ORCHESTRE IMPAIR

BEATLES

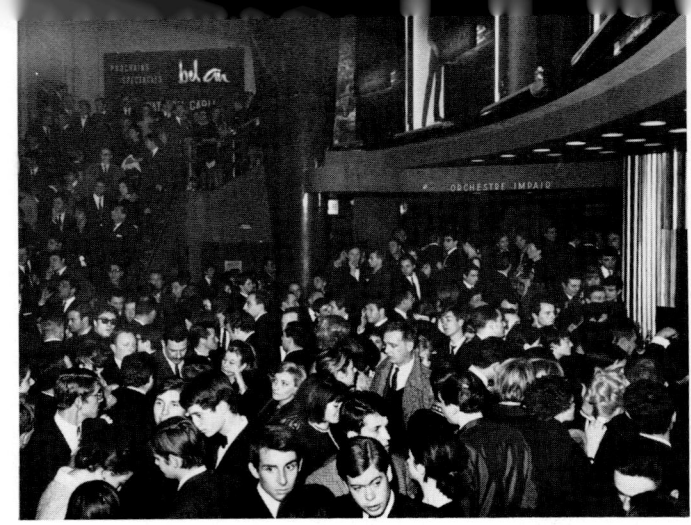

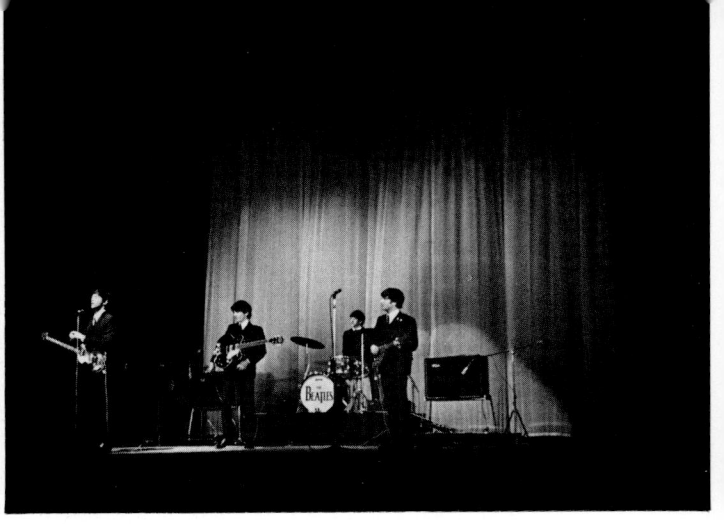

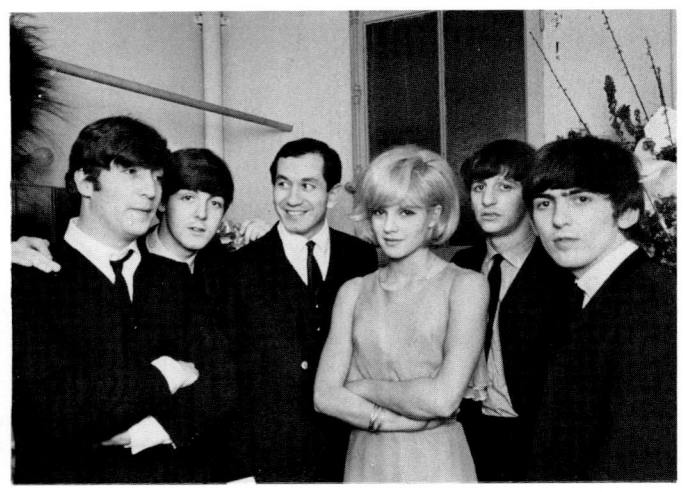

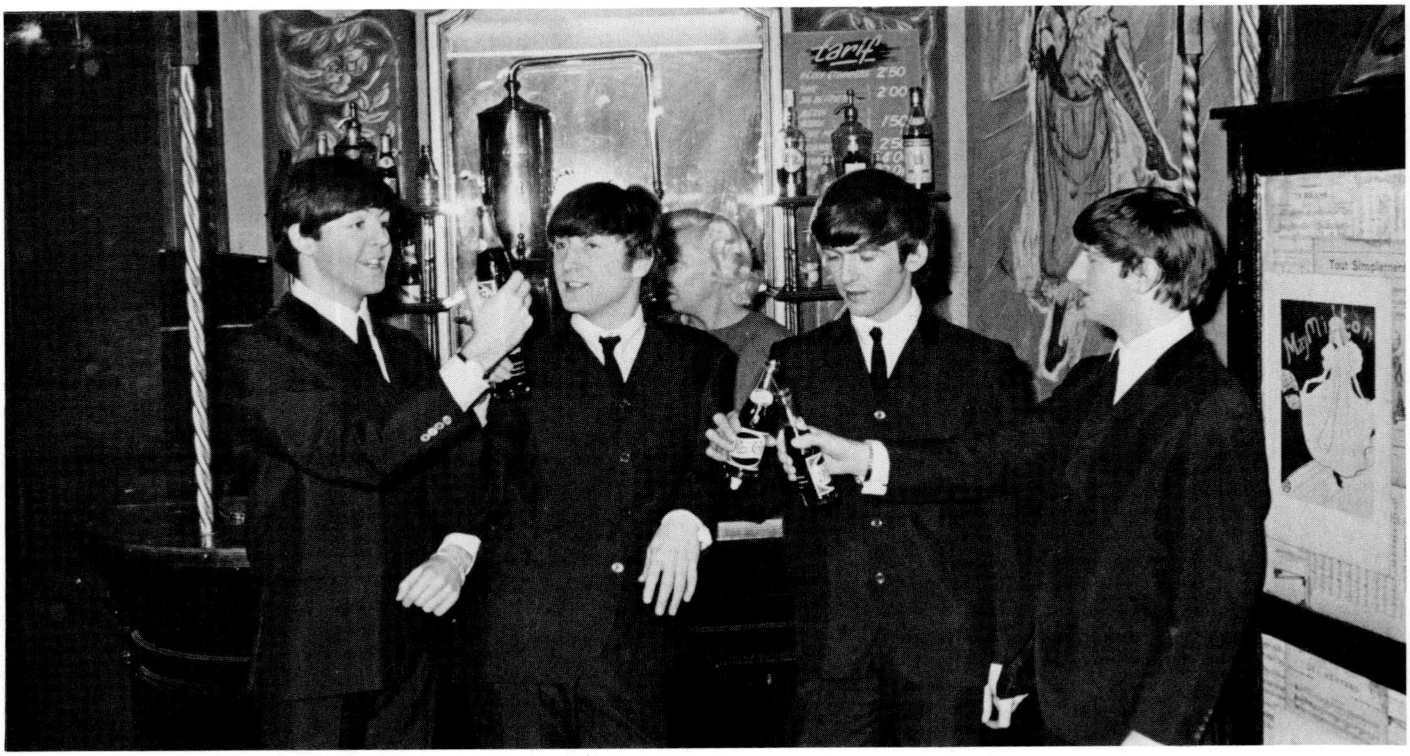
tarif

PARIS

PARIS

26

PARIS

NEW YORK

On the morning of the Beatles' flight to New York the VIP lounge at Heathrow was sheer pandemonium. It was a frenzy of activity, full of international journalists, radio and TV commentators, cine news cameramen and press photographers. In one corner conferring among themselves were Beatles Manager Brian Epstein, their music publisher from Northern Songs, Dick James and their producer George Martin. At the centre of attention were the Beatles, drinking tea and taking all the hustle and bustle completely for granted. Cynthia Lennon sat some distance away as if she didn't belong. It was only a few days since she had officially been acknowledged as a Beatle wife and we were still getting used to seeing this pretty young blond lady with the entourage.

The call for our flight was announced and we drifted sheepishly down on to the tarmac. Outside, we were stunned when we saw the size of the crowds; thousands of kids hanging off the terraces, pressed against the barriers, shrieking and waving goodbye, holding aloft banners and tender messages. The Beatles just grinned at each other, taking all the fuss and adulation in their stride. As they walked towards the plane I began taking pictures, trying to focus them in my viewfinder. The boys walked slowly in order to help me get the best shots. My assistant took pictures of me taking pictures of the Beatles and when I boarded the plane he took my rolls of film and rushed back to the studio to develop them.

Several businessmen were flying to New York with us solely to try and get a captive Brian Epstein to endorse their Beatle-related products. They were in tourist class with the press, while Brian and the boys were in first-class. It was so painful to see their requests continuously ignored that I suggested they go through the office of the Beatles' solicitor David Jacobs, the only avenue they'd left unexplored.

As we approached Kennedy airport we saw beneath us a vast swarm of people. We all thought President Johnson must be arriving. The plane circled lower and Phil Spector, the famous American record producer who was travelling with the Beatles in hope of doing even one record with them, had a pair of field glasses. He suddenly shouted "Look! Look! They're holding up Beatle banners!" This time the boys' cool faltered. Their mouths dropped open. Beatlemania had obviously exploded in the States.

The noise from the airport crowd was deafening. As we disembarked I was flabbergasted to see kids wearing white sweat-shirts with one of *my* Beatles pictures on the front. It wasn't until later that I found out the whole story behind those sweat-shirts. We passed smoothly through customs and passport control, and then it was time for the Beatles first American press reception.

The press room at Kennedy looked more like a huge aircraft hanger. At the front of the room was a long trestle table with four microphones. On a rostrum at the back there were cine and TV cameras. In between were crammed hundreds of reporters and photographers. I had one hell of a job moving around to take pictures. It was difficult getting long shots because of an overhanging cloud of haze; everyone seemed to be smoking cigars and the smoke added to the already electric atmosphere. It seemed as if one spark would blow the whole place up.

When Brian Sommerville's polite requests for order were ignored by the noisy mob, he simply shouted "Shut up!", which the Beatles echoed in their best scouse Sgt. Major voices. There was brief applause, then the whole place became like a church, so quiet you could hear the cameras clicking. No-one spoke out of turn; no-one said a word until Brian pointed to them. He had been an officer in the Royal Navy, and his military training showed.

Brian introduced the Beatles one by one, and the boys were in top form. They had the knack of being spontaneously funny, never taking anything too seriously. Every question got a witty answer. One by one the reporters fell for the Beatle charm. As soon as the Beatles US tour was announced, various anti-Beatle movements were formed against the long-haired invaders. I watched amazed as 200 hard-boiled reporters who'd come to destroy the Beatles ended up adoring them. The TV and radio wavelengths throughout the US buzzed with the Beatles' magnetism. It took just ten minutes for America to fall for the Beatles. It was the most unforgettable ten minutes of my life. In my mind, this is where they conquered America.

New York's Plaza Hotel was eventually persuaded to honour the Beatles' booking despite misgivings about safety. The hotel had become completely beseiged by fans, so the boys and their entourage were given the whole of the twelfth floor complete with special security arrangements. I fought my way outside, took some pictures of the crowd, fought my way back inside, found my luggage, and went upstairs. The boys were all flopped out on their beds, jet-lagged and aching after the longest flight and most important press reception they'd ever endured. Still, despite their fatigue, I am certain the boys sensed that they were on their way to incredible success. They weren't afraid of massive fame; on the contrary, they were very ready for it. I took a few more pictures to capture the atmosphere of the aftermath of the arrival, then went to bed, exhausted. Later that evening Ringo mustered the energy to sneak out and visit the famous Peppermint Lounge, 'Home of the Twist', and wasn't even recognised.

The next morning George woke up with a throat infection. His sister Louise had arrived from Illinois and looked after him, insisting he stay in bed. George was in no condition to argue.

The rehearsal for the first Ed Sullivan show wasn't scheduled until that afternoon, so to please the press we decided to go out for a photo-call in nearby Central Park. We arrived at the boat house where the photographers were already waiting, and enough photographs must have been taken that morning to make a feature film. Pictorially, the session turned out to be a classic.

That afternoon we travelled to the CBS-TV studios on 53rd Street in limousines escorted by about forty mounted police, wielding their batons and very skillfully maneuvering the kids that were blocking the street. After the Sullivan crew and the Beatles' entourage were introduced to each other, it was decided a George substitute was needed for visual technicalities such as lighting and camera angles. A production assistant in a Beatle wig stood in, but then Sullivan himself insisted "a real English boy" be used. Road manager Neil Aspinall was chosen, and became George Harrison for the duration of the rehearsal.

It was a happy occasion. Everyone was impressed and pleased with each other, the Beatles by the efficiency of the Sullivan people and the ingenuity of the original sets designed for them and the CBS crew by the Beatles' professionalism. A mutual admiration society had developed.

The following day, February 9th, the boys were scheduled to be at the CBS studio all day for a dress rehearsal, a taping for another Sullivan show, and finally for the first live TV broadcast of the Beatles in America. George's condition was touch-and-go; bulletins on his health were broadcast hourly nationwide and church services prayed for his recovery. (It was, after all, a Sunday). I shared the limo with him on the way to the studio. He was well wrapped up with scarves. Still running a high temperature, he insisted on singing, so CBS called in a doctor who administered enough medicines and vitamins to keep him going.

The boys treated the dress rehearsal like a proper performance, much to the delight of the carefully-chosen audience. The stage sets were changed for both the taping and the live performance. I thought that eventually George would lose his voice – but he didn't. He drank lots of liquids and in his excitement, with all the extra adrenalin flowing, he completely overcame his bad throat.

The next day a high-ranking police officer came to see Brian and congratulated him and the Beatles on an astonishing drop in crime in America; on the evening of February 9th, 1964, while seventy million people watched the Ed Sullivan Show, America's crime rate plunged dramatically to the lowest figure for fifty years.

While we were staying at the Plaza, I met Nicky Byrne, one of the partners in the Beatles merchandising company Selteab, and he told me the story behind the Beatles' sweat-shirts: It seems that some weeks before he'd overheard a distraught American businessman in the Plaza bar complaining he'd just bought two wagonloads of white ex-army track-suits on the cheap, but was now having second thoughts about how easy it would be to get rid of them. Byrne had been worried that Capitol Records weren't doing enough to promote the Beatles' forthcoming visit and was working on promotional ideas of his own. There and then, Byrne had a brainwave and persuaded the businessman to part with some of the track-suit tops at 50 cents apiece, payable later. Byrne then had my now-famous picture of the Beatles sharing a chair silk-screened to the front in two-colour black and grey. It looked rather nice, but no-one had asked my permission. Byrne had then found two high schools in the Bronx and bribed the kids with an offer they couldnt refuse: $1 each, free travel to the airport and a free sweat-shirt. He had also advertised the sweat-shirt and dollar-bill deal on two radio stations. *That* was why I saw all those kids at the airport and outside the Plaza with my photo on their chest.

I later stumbled across an uncomfortable incident at the Plaza. I knocked on Brian Epstein's door and opened it to find Sommerville crying like a baby and Epstein shouting at him as if he were a complete idiot, telling him to go home on the next plane. I beat a retreat, and soon Sommerville came out to tell me what had happened. It seemed Epstein was in a temper because a newspaper had quoted Brian Sommerville as being spokesman for the Beatles, and Epstein thought *he* should be the spokesman. I went and spoke to Epstein and very diplomatically told him to make up the quarrel. I had to justify it very carefully, saying "You can't be spokesman, you are above all that, you should be glad you have a good press officer." He must have taken my point, because he went to Sommerville's room and apologised.

The press conference at the Plaza ballroom was held on February 10th and to Brian Sommerville's relief he had a microphone all to himself, which saved him from a sore throat. Due to all the film and TV lighting I was not satisfied with my pictures. I don't use flash and I couldn't make use of the film and TV lighting because it concentrated only on the Beatles themselves. I wanted to capture not only the Beatles but the atmosphere throughout the magnificent room. Whenever I found some nice even light, someone would spoil it for me by pointing light on the Beatles, so that it was nearly impossible to get a shot of the entire room without washing out the Beatles.

By this time the boys had perfected their ad-lib dialogue with the press, never giving a straight answer. What stands out most in my mind even today is how well Sommerville once again controlled the massed ranks of the world's top media.

After two and a half hours of questions, the Beatles were frantic with hunger. John had the bright idea of loudly requesting food over his microphone, and in a matter of minutes a waiter brought along a silver platter stacked with roast chicken and the famous little Plaza rolls. He plonked it down in front of the boys and everything disappeared in seconds.

PAGE 34

In the VIP lounge at Heathrow. Standing at the back of the boys, left to right, are Brian Epstein, lawyer David Jacobs, and the chauffeur who drove them around Paris. Jacobs was a world-famous divorce laywer with offices in London and LA. The Beatles never dreamed of going to America and until this point never aimed their music at the American market. John said, "I feel just like those old European émigrés setting off to the promised land!" *For the Beatles, playing music was a pleasure, not work. This trip was the icing on the cake.*

PAGE 35

Top: *Cynthia Lennon had been sitting all alone like a Cinderella, terribly shy, in a corner of the VIP lounge until John went over and asked a waiter to bring her refreshments. At that time, nobody know who she was. In the left of this picture is Hungarian-born Jussy Antall, London editor of the Swedish newspaper* Expressen. **Centre:** *Paul posing with a sandwich and his customary glass of milk.* **Bottom:** *Killing time before take-off by polishing up on their spontaneous banter with the journalists. It also helped take their minds off the Atlantic crossing, which they dreaded.*

PAGE 36

Top: *In the first-class cabin of Pan-Am Flight 101 Jet Clipper 'Defiance', Paul pretends to be an inaccessible big shot: "No photographs please".* **Bottom left:** *Waiting on the tarmac in his uniform of dark glasses and little cap is American record producer Phil Spector, then red-hot with world-wide hits by his groups the Crystals, the Ronettes, Bob B. Soxx & the Bluejeans and Darlene Love. Spector had been in London on business with Decca Records, and he flew back to the US on the same flight as the Beatles, assessing his chances of producing them. His ambitions in that direction weren't fulfilled until 1970 when he got to produce their last album, 'Let It Be.' Next to Phil is photographer Robert Freeman, who was responsible for several early Beatles' record sleeve photos.* **Bottom right:** *The press were tipped off about the arrival of Mr and Mrs John Lennon, seen here unsuccessfully sneaking into a back entrance at Heathrow.*

PAGE 37

Top: *The protocol in Great Britain dictates that the press must never walk in front of the sovereign. At Kennedy airport I was more privileged; the New York authorities let me walk in front of the procession of police and customs officials escorting the Fab Four towards custom and passport control areas.* **Bottom left and right:** *The customs search very light-hearted. In between looking through the boys' luggage, the normally sternfaced customs officers managed to persuade the Beatles to sign plenty of autographs.*

PAGE 38

Top: *In the press lounge at Kennedy Airport where the most important press conference of the Beatles' career took place. This shot was taken at the beginning of the conference with the boys still looking a little perturbed before warming up for their triumph. The extended arm of Brian Sommerville points to the lucky reporter chosen to ask a question. Sommerville handled the whole affair with the aplomb of a maestro conductor controlling his own orchestra.* **Bottom:** *Paul appears quite self-assured now the ice has been broken.*

PAGE 39

Top: *This is only a small section of the press and TV reporters gathered at the Kennedy press lounge. You can see the effect of the Beatles on the faces of the hard-bitten journalists and camera crews from all over the world.* **Bottom:** *On the roads outside the airport terminal every available space was filled with fans. Police and airport guards were everywhere, keeping back the crowds and making sure the airwaves were not disturbed with too many of the personal walkie-talkies that American reporters used to contact their offices.*

PAGES 40 & 41

Outside the Plaza Hotel where we nearly didn't get in. On the whole, the crowds were well-behaved and did what the police requested, letting hotel guests and visitors pass through and making way for the convoys of taxis. **Page 40:** *Note the fans wearing the sweat-shirts bearing my Beatles photo.*

PAGES 42 & 43

The walkabout in Central Park. George was sick, but the others enjoyed themselves hugely. In those days, Central Park was said to be a lot safer. **Page 42, Top:** *View from John's bedroom at the Plaza. You can see the skaters on the ice-rink, and surrounding the park are some of the most exclusive and expensive apartment buildings in America.*

PAGES 44 & 45

Naturally, the boys had to have a ride on one of Central Park's famous horse-drawn carriages.

PAGE 46

Top: *En route from the Plaza to CBS-TV Studios on 53rd street. Protection of the Beatles was a fantastic accomplishment by the New York Police Department. Unfortunately, I didn't have a wide-angle lense to capture what was happening on both sides of the street where the crowds were being continuously pushed back by the mounted police.* **Bottom:** *Outside the CBS-TV studios. Note the all-British line-up for the upcoming Ed Sullivan Show.*

PAGE 47

Top: *Brian and Ed Sullivan discuss technicalities.* **Bottom:** *Brian tells John he has just received a phone call from George's sister Louise saying her brother will definitely not be attending today's rehearsal.*

PAGE 48

Top: *Paul explains to Ed Sullivan the intricacies of his left-handed bass guitar.* **Bottom:** *With the show's floor manager, cueing for the correct camera angles.*

PAGE 49

Top: *Working out the technical aspects of the show. The floor of the studio was very shiny and slippery, kept clean by the guy at the back of the picture who continuously swept up.* **Bottom:** *As if there weren't enough camera complications, Ringo grabbed one of mine and started to photograph Paul. By this time most of their worries about the show had vanished, and they were settling into enjoying the whole occasion.*

PAGE 50

Rehearsing without George. **Bottom:** *Ed insists that "an English boy" is substituted for absent George, and Neil Aspinall puts on the lead guitar. Out went the Sullivan technician with the Beatle wig who had been George for a few magic minutes.*

PAGE 51

Top: *Neil Aspinall in the rehearsal line-up.* **Bottom left:** *George with his sister Louise. She was very proud of her baby brother and came all the way from Illinois to meet him in New York. She ended up nursing him during his brief illness.* **Bottom right:** *For Ringo, a rehearsal was no different to the show itself.*

PAGE 52

Part of the vast amount of Beatles' merchandising items which swept Britain and America, all using my photographs. Note the colour poster of the boys in old-fashioned Edwardian bathing costumes, taken at Weston-Super-Mare the previous summer with the American market in mind. It was the very first pop poster, a piece of pop merchandise now taken for granted. The wallpaper was manufact-

ured by the Crown wallpaper company. An amazing amount of Britain's teenagers had their rooms decorated with it.

PAGE 53
The Beatles' own postroom at the Plaza was a hastily-converted spare bedroom on the 12th floor. At least six sackloads of mail arrived daily and were sorted out by two girls from the American fan club, helped by occasional visits from the boys themselves to encourage them. The gentleman in the background is a security officer

PAGE 54
Top: Lining up with Ed Sullivan for the televised trailer for the first New York show; note the army of photographers lurking behind. **Bottom:** The trailer broadcast is over and the boys turn around to face the photographers.

PAGE 55
Top: This is the way they looked to viewers all over America on the show's trailer. **Bottom left:** Holding up Ed Sullivan's prompting card for a trailer of the attractions on the forthcoming Miami show. **Bottom right:** John was so short-sighted he couldn't read the prompter and wrote down his lines on a small piece of paper instead. Later, just before the live broadcast, he wrote them down again, – on his hand.

PAGES 56 & 57
Lining up for CBS-TV's promotional shots. These are roughly the same images that were captured by the 10" × 8" plate camera.

PAGE 58
Photographers from the more privileged papers stayed behind for these onstage 'working shots'.

PAGE 59
Dress rehearsal shots. **Bottom right:** After the rehearsal the boys loosen up.

PAGE 60
The live broadcast itself. Note the clever use of perspective in the set, creating the illusion of a fantastically deep studio.

PAGE 61
I thought it would be more interesting to photograph the younger section of the show's audience, most of whom were seated up in the balcony.

PAGE 62
This was the show taped for broadcast the week after the Miami performance. The Beatles were very impressed by the ingenuity of the Sullivan show's art department.

PAGE 63
Top: Waiting around during the editing of the taped show. **Bottom:** Warm congratulations from Sullivan for Beatles' co-star Tessie O'Shea. She proved such a success with American audiences that she stayed in the US permanently.

PAGE 64
Top: Back in their Plaza suite, John, Paul and George share a joke with Murray the K. I think my Astrakhan hat went to Murray's head. **Bottom:** The Phil Spector connection. Murray the K brought along one of the Ronettes to the Plaza suite, interviewing her along with the Beatles on a live radio broadcast.

PAGE 65
Top: One of the many hundreds of interviews the Beatles gave in their hotel suites. **Bottom:** Using their home-made 16mm movie camera, one of the Maysles Brothers films Paul and Ringo, while the other brother holds the microphone at the right of the picture.

PAGE 66
Top: One of the great personal joys of the Beatles was to be acclaimed in the country from where most of their musical inspiration had sprung. They took full advantage of their new-found power by getting free boxes of records from all the record companies in New York. **Bottom:** Paul tries on a Beatles hat.

PAGE 67
John and Ringo proudly pose with their precious gold discs.

PAGE 68
One room on their floor at the Plaza was full of presents, mainly sweets and chocolates, which made a good sugar substitute for the Parisian crepes they missed so much.

PAGE 69
Bottom: Ringo being interviewed live on air from the Plaza. On this particular occasion he was being very funny, and everyone in the suite was falling about laughing.

PAGES 70 & 71
These shots of the boys posing for Newsweek are rather static. They weren't used to this kind of formal photography.

PAGE 72
Top: Everyone and his wife wanted to be photographed with a Beatle. This shot was taken at the end of the Plaza press conference. **Bottom:** At the Plaza press conference: "Just one last shot together, boys!"

PAGE 73
Top: Nationally televised psychologist Dr Joyce Brothers met the Beatles during the Plaza press conference and later wrote an interesting analysis of their appeal. Here the boys turn the tables on her, – John attracts her attention while Ringo feels her pulse. **Bottom:** Re-enacting one of the scenes from the Paris Match photo spread, this time with an American reporter dressed in a Beatle wig. "Do I really look like that?" muses George.

PAGE 74
Part of the Baroque Rooms used for the Plaza press conference. You can see the increased proportion of women journalists compared with the earlier press reception at Kennedy.

PAGE 75
Top: Eating the long-awaited chicken after several gruelling hours in front of the international media at the Plaza. **Bottom:** Polite smiles during the gold disc presentation ceremony at the Plaza by Capitol's Alan Livingstone.

PAGES 76 & 77
After the main question time at the conference it was everyone for themselves. The reporters zoomed in for their individual quotes from the individual Beatles. It was absolute chaos.

NEW YORK

NEW YORK

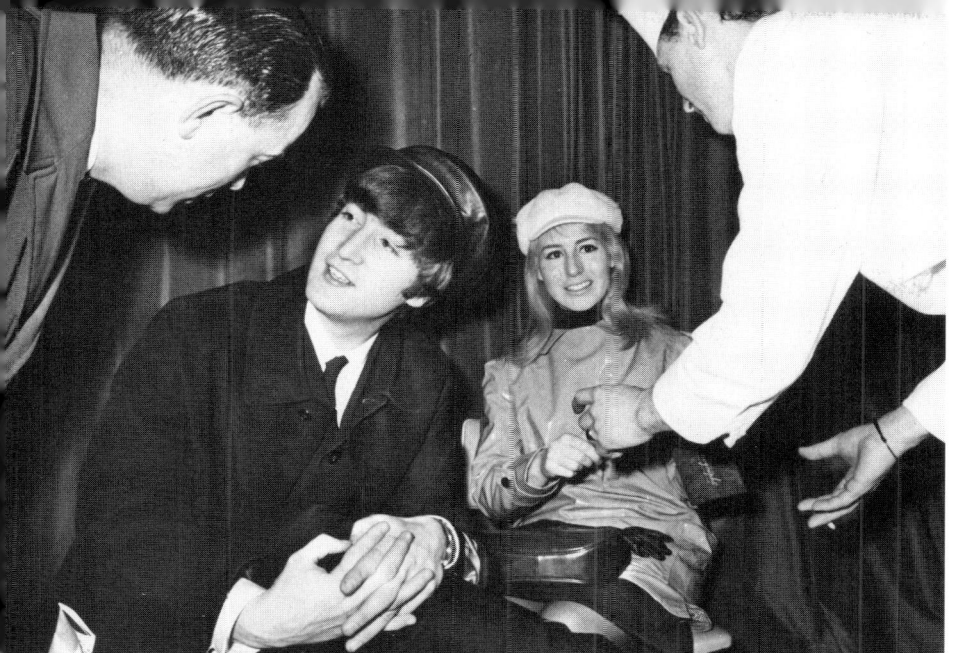

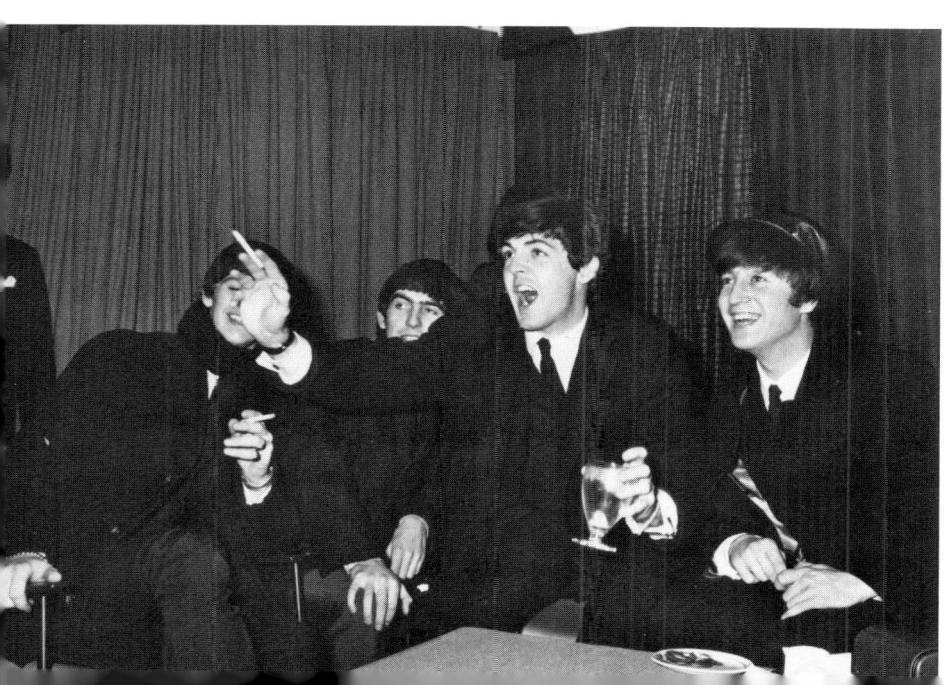

NEW YORK

NEW YORK

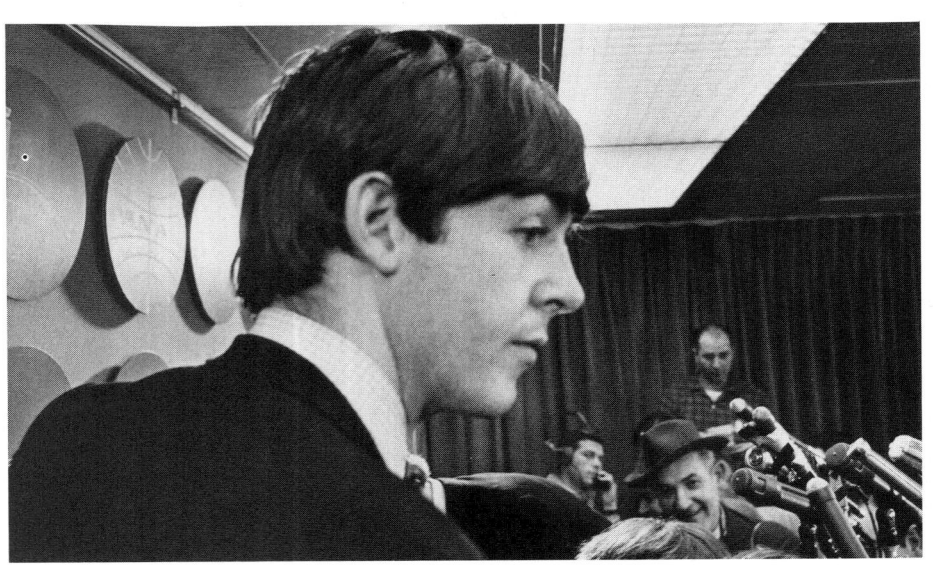

38

NEW YORK

NEW YORK

NEW YORK

NEW YORK

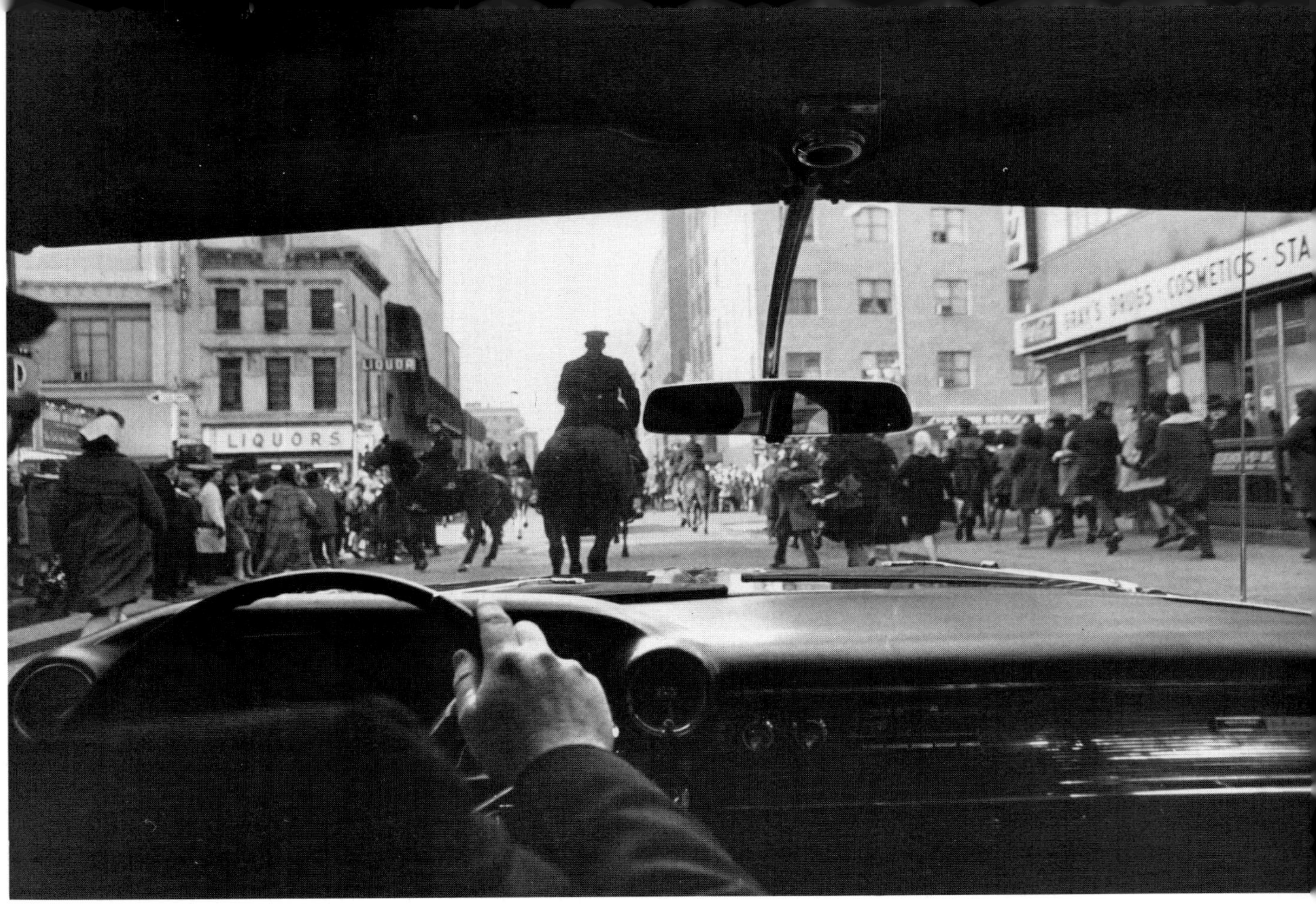
LIQUORS
LIQUOR
GRAY'S DRUGS - COSMETICS - STA

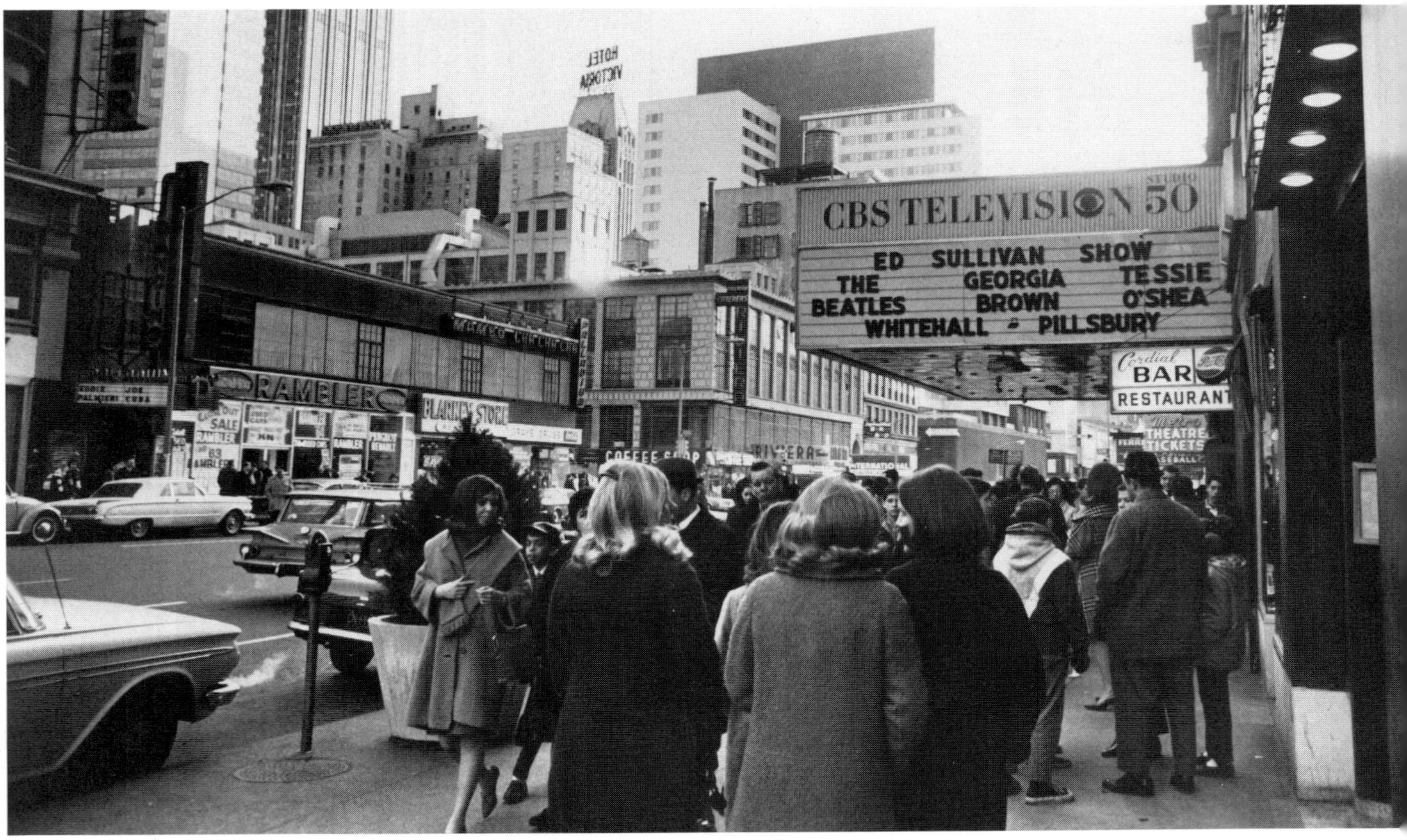
HOTEL VICTORIA
CBS TELEVISION 50
STUDIO
ED SULLIVAN SHOW
THE BEATLES
GEORGIA BROWN
TESSIE O'SHEA
WHITEHALL
PILLSBURY
RAMBLER
Cordial BAR
RESTAURANT
THEATRE TICKETS

NEW YORK

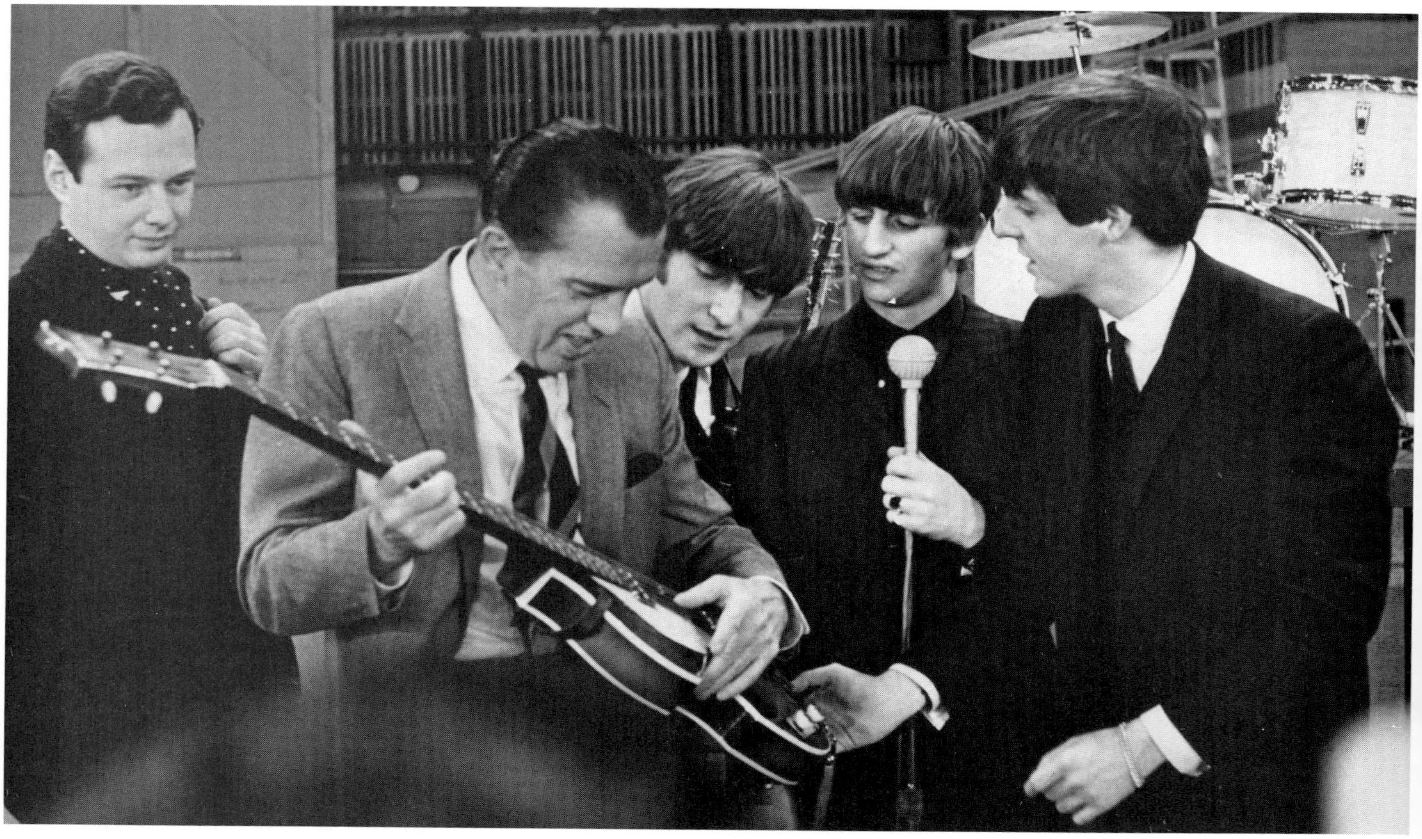

NEW YORK

NEW YORK

NEW YORK

51

NEW YORK

53

ED
MITZI GAYNOR, THE BEATLES,
COMEDY STARS MYRON COHEN,
ALLEN AND ROSSI HEADLINE
OUR SHOW FROM MIAMI BEACH

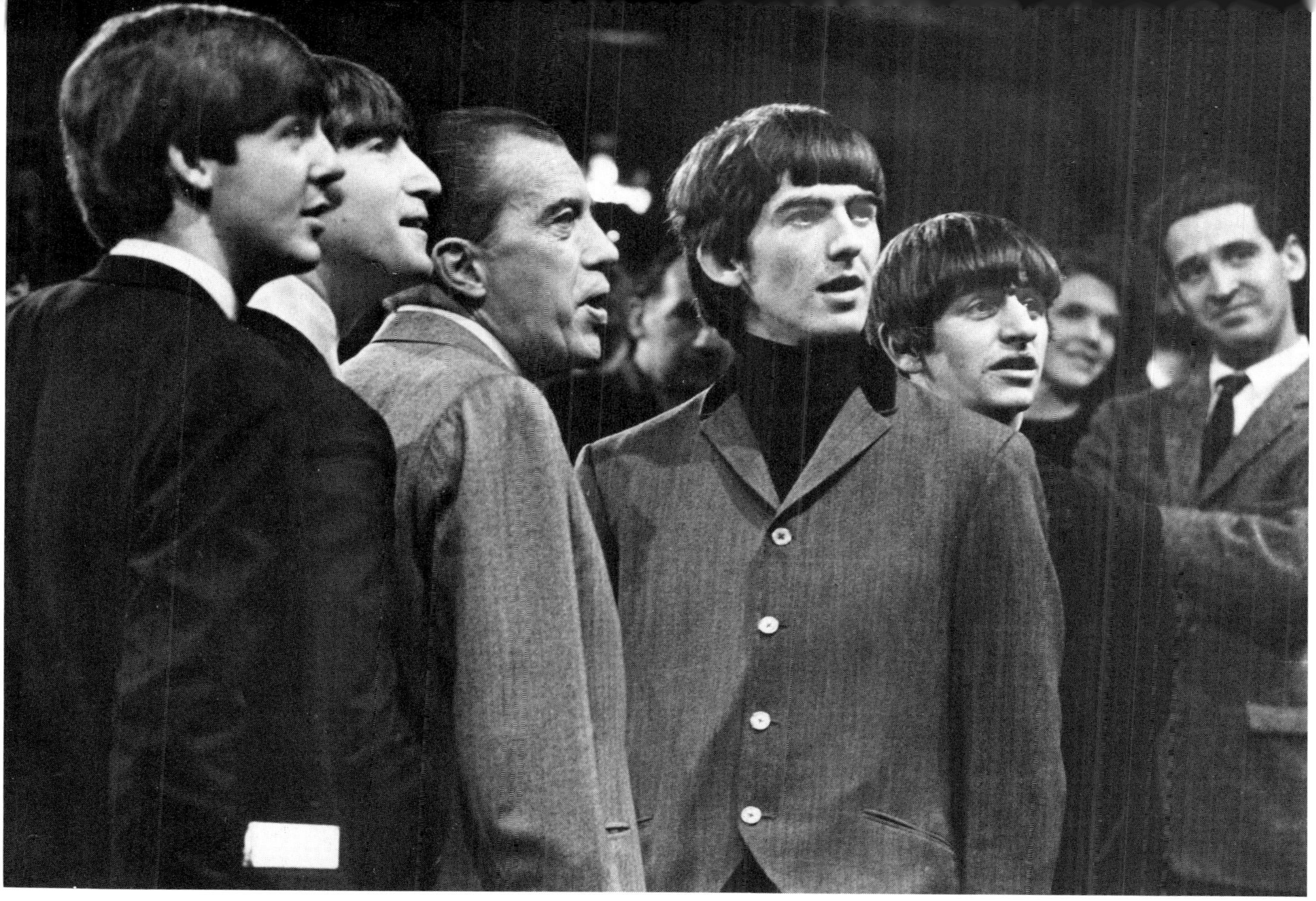

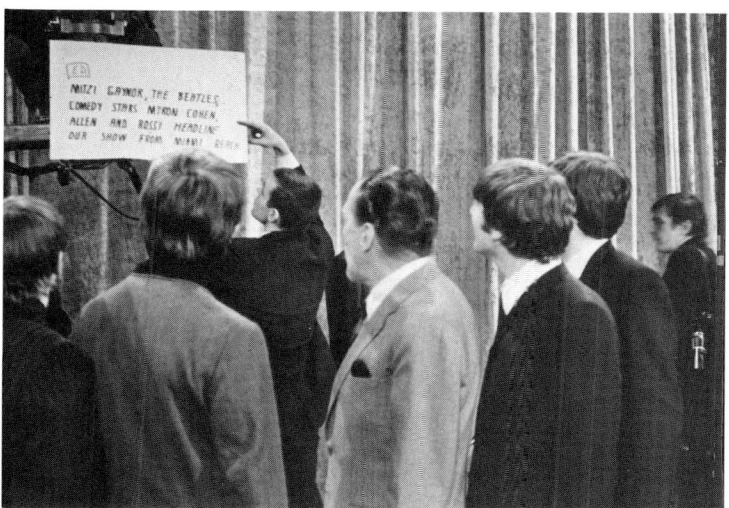

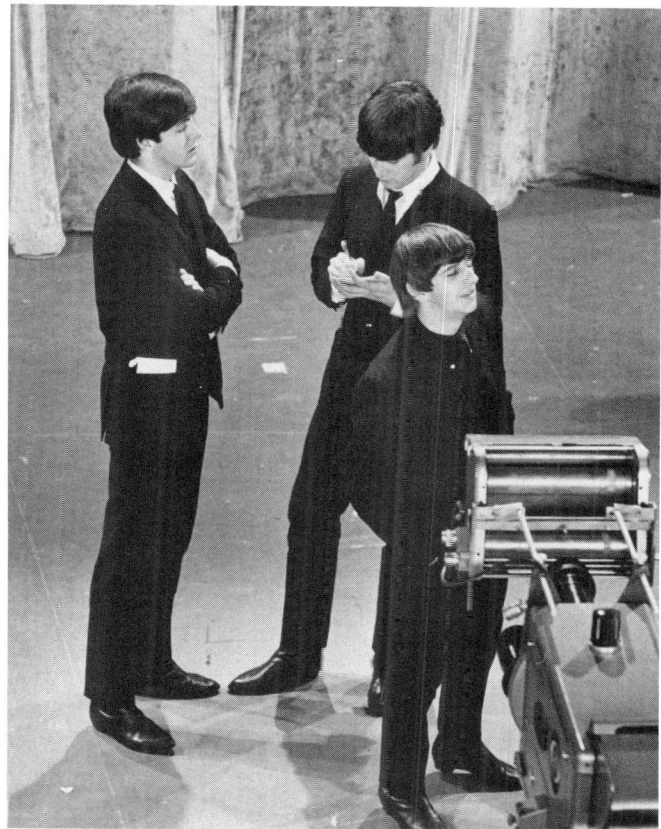

NEW YORK

56

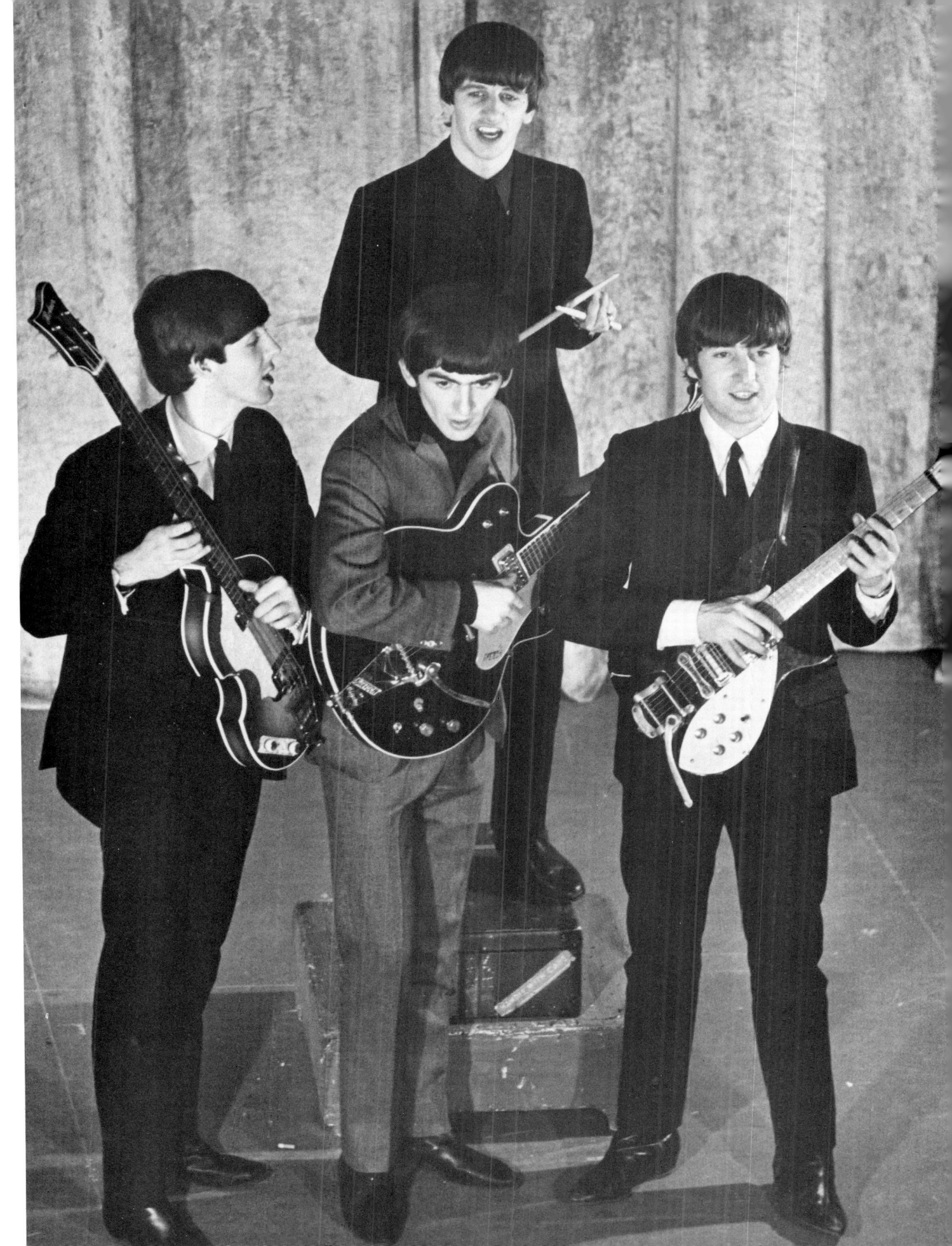

NEW YORK

NEW YORK

NEW YORK

NEW YORK

NEW YORK

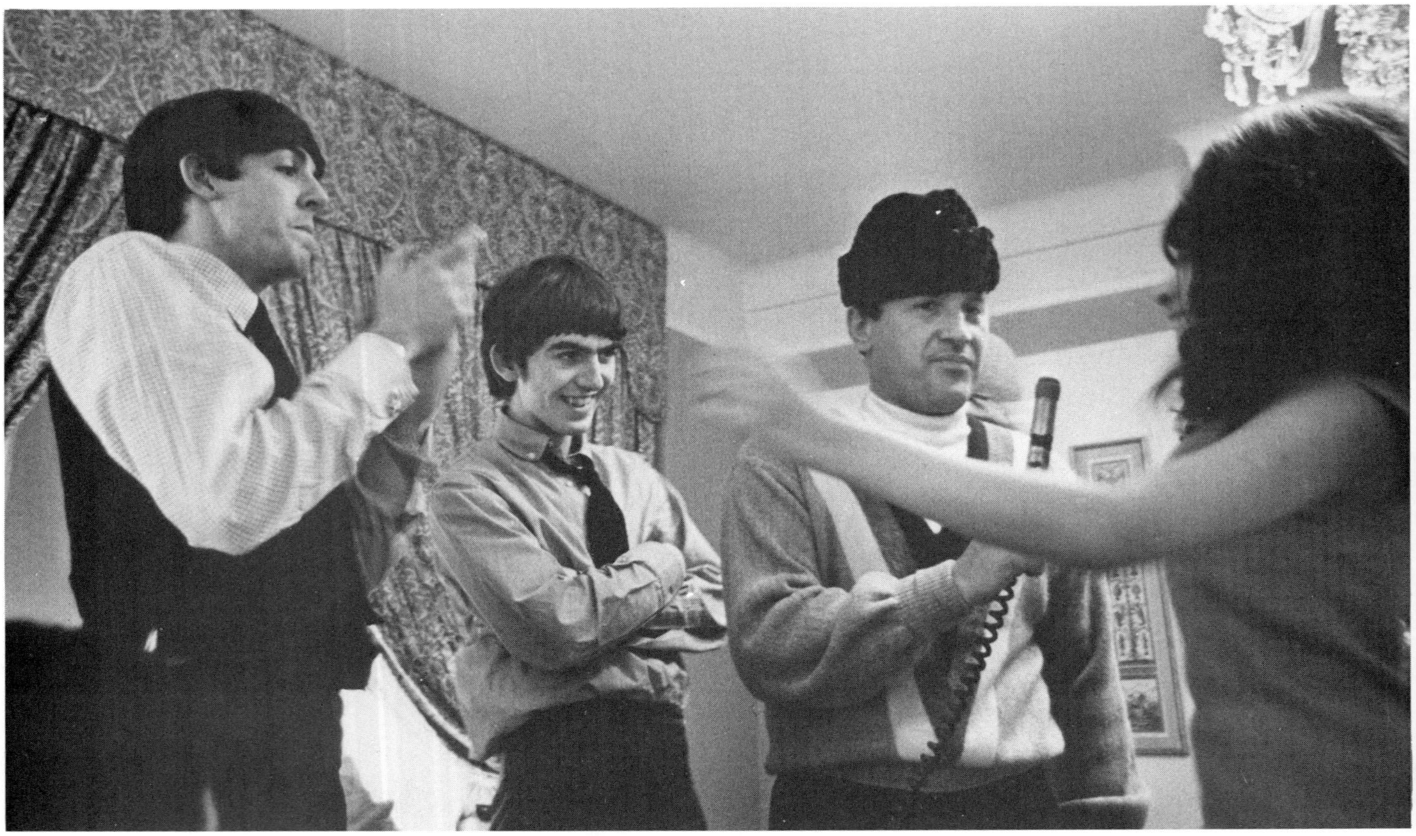

NEW YORK

NEW YORK

66

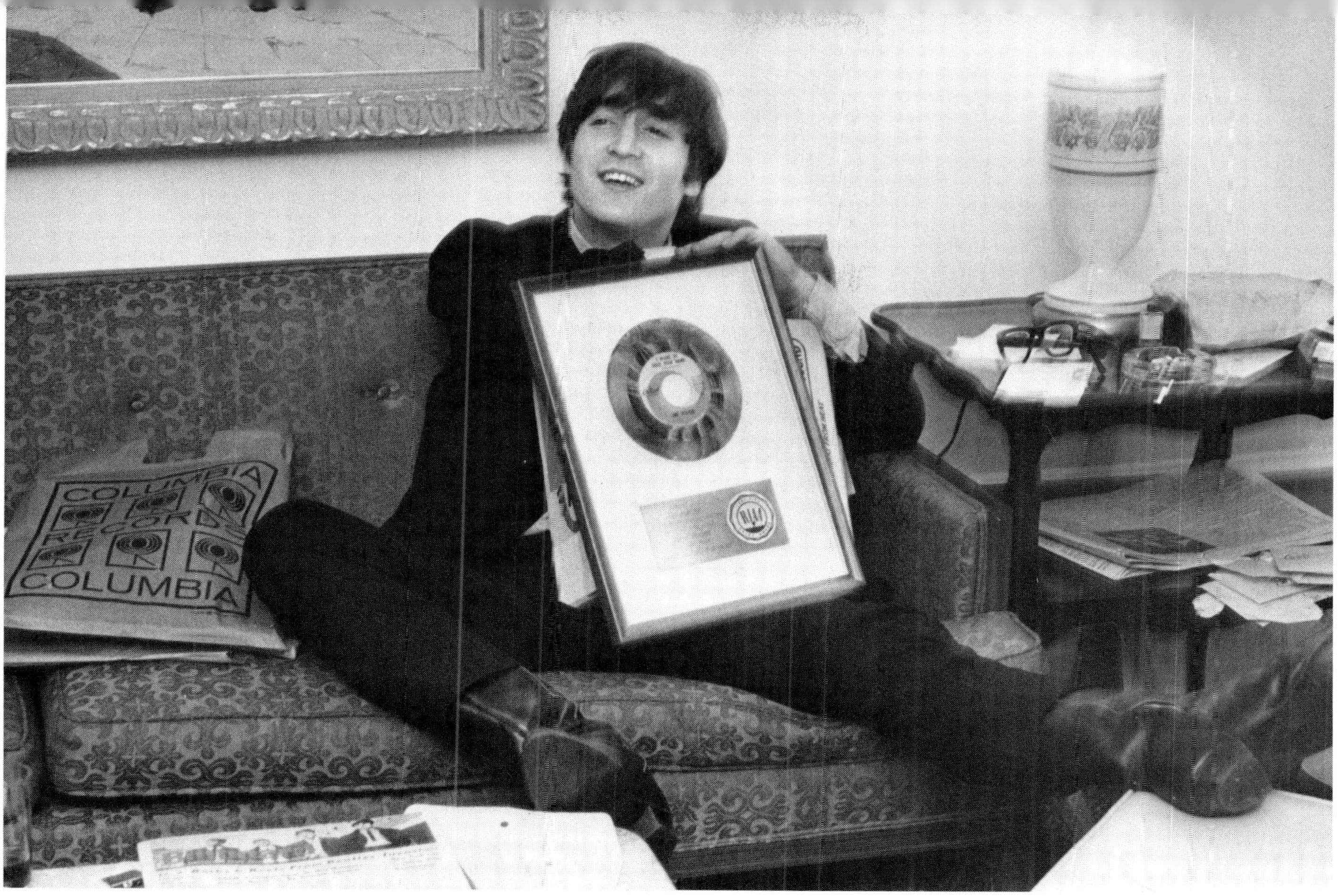
COLUMBIA
RECORDS
COLUMBIA

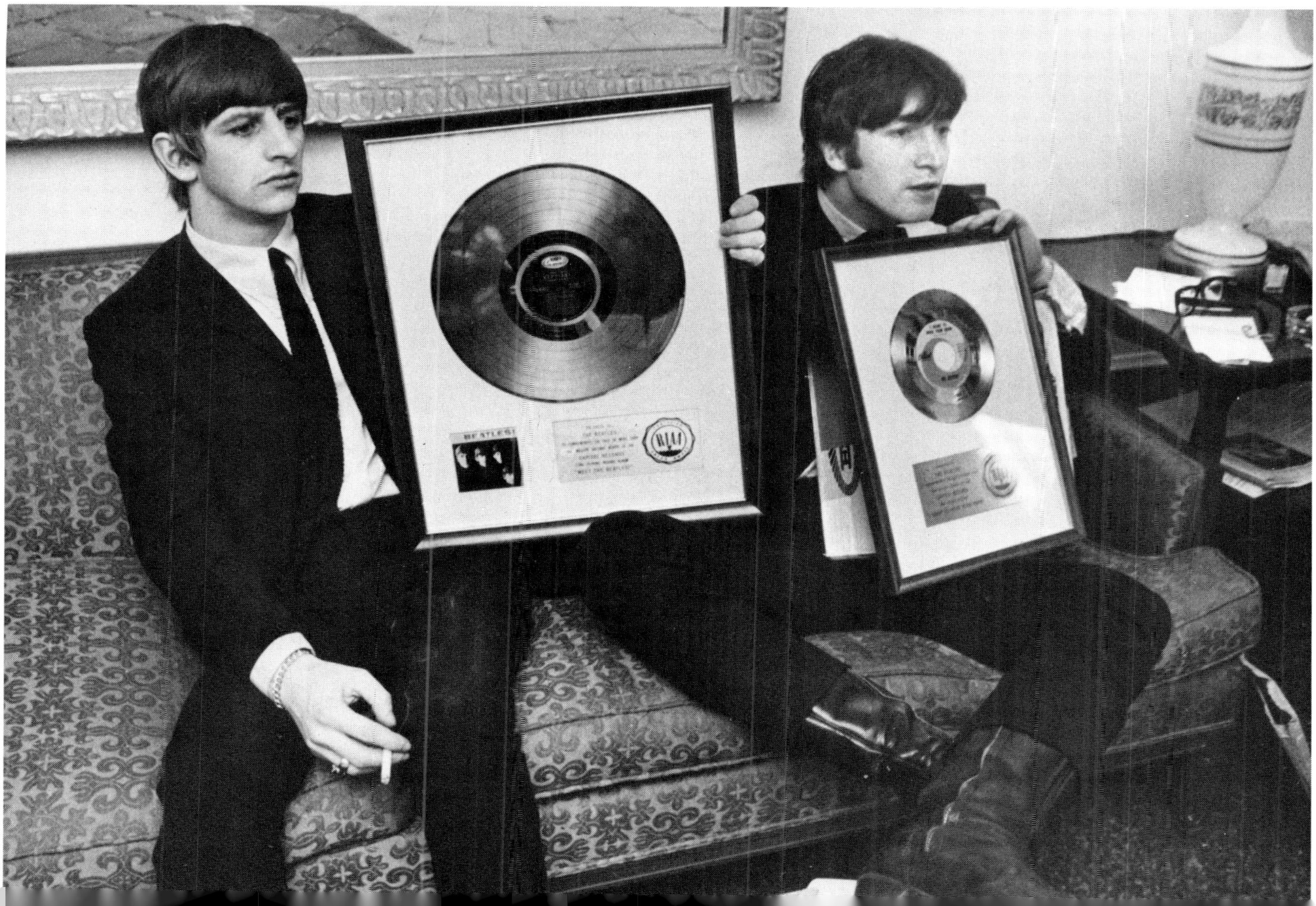
BEATLES!

NEW YORK

NEW YORK

71

NEW YORK

72

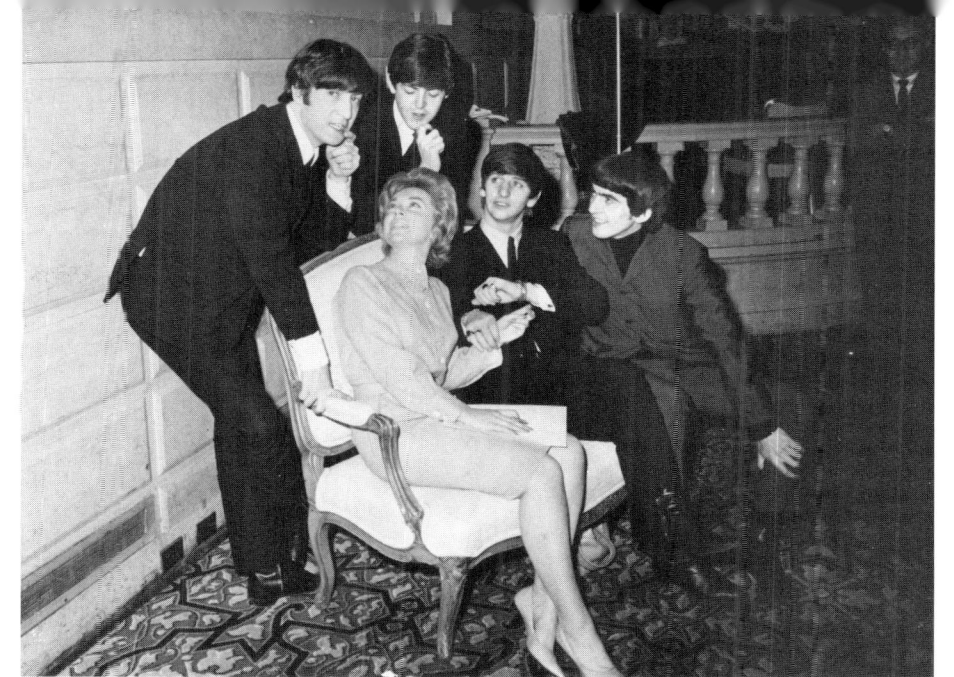

NEW YORK

NEW YORK

NEW YORK

WASHINGTON DC

So small was the fee paid to the Beatles for their Sullivan Show appearances – "the greatest three-thousand dollar investment in the history of American television", as Brian Epstein, put it that in order to offset their losses on the trip, a hastily-arranged concert was set up in Washington DC.

February 11th was set to be one of the busiest days in the whole two-week itinerary. The Beatles were due to fly to Washington for a press reception, for their first actual concert in America, and for a ball at the British Embassy. I woke up that morning in New York, opened the curtains and nearly died. Thick snow had fallen all night and was still falling. I phoned Brian Sommerville's room to give him the weather report. By the time we met up with the boys, everyone had seen the snow.

The Beatles flatly refused to fly. Five years earlier to the month, their idol Buddy Holly had died in a plane crash during a snowstorm and now the Beatles didn't trust American pilots, particularly in snowstorms. Alternative transport was needed, so for the next hour, Brian Sommerville, Brian Epstein and his new assistant Wendy Hanson co-ordinated a three-telephone operation to make the necessary arrangements with the railroad. The results proved excellent; a magnificent old luxury sleeper was to be added on to the end of a regular New York-Washington DC train scheduled to arrive by early afternoon. It would give us ample time for everything.

I grabbed my cameras and overnight case and we all piled into taxis and headed for Pennsylvania Station. The railroad authorities made sure we avoided the fans by shunting us through a series of back doors and down through elevators until we arrived at a goods platform where we could board the train. I felt a bit sorry for the masses of fans who had missed seeing the Beatles – and even sorrier for the fans waiting at the airport who hadn't heard about the change of arrangements.

The train journey was a most memorable event. There were transistor radios in the carriage and every station was either playing Beatles records, broadcasting Beatle interviews, or announcing news about the Beatles! Ringo listened until he couldn't stand it anymore and became a photographer for the rest of the trip. All the boys had a go with my cameras at one time or another, but Ringo seemed to have the most natural ability and became quite good.

The train was very fast, which added to the lively atmosphere. The carriage was equipped with armchair seats that swivelled and reclined. It was a press photographers' paradise because the Beatles couldn't escape! True to form, they played around for the cameras, circulated with the reporters and DJs and found time to talk to everybody. Other passengers on the train sometimes came along and peeped in at them.

The entourage was split into little groups and this caused some confusion among the press. No-one really knew who Cynthia was. She added to the confusion by putting on and taking off a black wig and dark glasses. Most of the Americans thought that Cynthia and Judy, George Martin's fiancée, were groupies! George Martin himself was probably the busiest person on the train; the American reporters could understand his beautifully spoken English far more easily than the Beatles' Liverpool brogue.

George's sister Louise was traveling with us at this time. She was quite a novelty, because previous to this American trip no-one knew that George even had a sister. She was a very pleasant lady but didn't sit much with George on the journey. She spent most of her time talking to the other Beatles, especially Paul.

When the train pulled in at Washington's Union Station, I fought my way to the front of the crowd of reporters and photographers and began walking backwards so I could photograph the whole entourage coming towards me. The crush grew thicker, with reporters' microphones and police batons all waving in the air together. With the steam rising and the snow and the crowd, it all somehow reminded me of a Russian movie.

Outside the station 3,000 Beatlemaniacs were being held back by the 20-foot platform gates. The railroad authorities weren't letting any fans onto the platform. As we all moved slowly out of the station, up trotted Carroll James, the WWDC DJ who first started playing 'I Want To Hold Your Hand' and who would be compering the concert that evening. He had prepared limousines for our getaway to the press reception at the Coliseum. The snowploughs had already been out and mountains of snow were piled up along the sides of the streets. We raced through the slush with a police escort.

The Coliseum was a huge enclosed sports stadium, so dark inside we could hardly see a thing after the blinding snow. As our eyes became accustomed to the light we noticed a smallish platform in the centre with amplifiers and microphones positioned on it. This was where the press conference would be held. We were a bit surprised because we'd expected a room, not the whole hall!

Brian Sommerville was at a loss as to how to conduct this conference, especially as we couldn't see many journalists, but when Carroll James called for more houselights to be switched on, we realised a lot of people were already waiting for us. We also noticed many more journalists, DJs, photographers and film crews filing into the stadium behind us. They had all been waiting in the warmth of nearby cafes, peering out of the window every so often until we arrived, not wanting to stand in the bleak cold of the stadium any longer than necessary. Media from all over the world was represented. A diplomat from the British Embassy was there to offer the boys help with any passport or visa problems and to officially invite them to a party that evening.

Brian Sommerville introduced the boys to the press, who began shooting questions in many different languages, everyone wanting something original. I was in a terrible state because the place was still comparatively dark and I wanted to capture the vastness of the stadium. I had to take time-exposures with a hand-held camera in order to get the result I was after. We didn't stay too long; the place was like a refrigerator and the media people were frozen stiff. Everyone was anxious to get to the warmth of the hotel.

When we arrived at the Shoreham Hotel, a charming gentleman was waiting on the steps to greet us, enquiring which of our party was Dezo Hoffmann. I didn't know why he wanted me, but it turned out he was a Hungarian refugee from the 1956 uprising and was now assistant hotel manager. "With a name like Dezo," he told me, "I knew you could only be from our part of the world." This was a cause for celebration, and my fellow-countryman made sure we were all installed in splendid suites with a cold buffet and drinks in every room.

Unbeknowst to the Beatles, a space problem had arisen because one family refused to move out of the seventh floor in order to make room for the entourage. The assistant manager was worried that the family might be disturbed when the boys returned to the hotel after the concert to celebrate. The hotel management solved the problem during the concert. They staged a fake power failure on the seventh floor, cutting off light, heat and water, and offered the family a much nicer suite on the fifth floor. They took it. We didn't even know about this incident until the next day on the platform at Union Station. The assistant manager came along to see us off and just casually mentioned it.

We arrived for the concert later that day and my earlier impression of the Coliseum as a big empty warehouse was shattered. It was now bathed in light and the wooden seats crammed with thousands of excited kids. The noise was simply incredible and it was nearly impossible to get near the stage. Luckily a friendly policeman realised my predicament and escorted me to a favourable vantage point.

The supporting acts, including Tommy Roe and the Chiffons, were continually drowned out by waves of screams that shook the auditorium whenever a new rumour about the Beatles flashed through the crowd. When the Chiffons left the stage the noise built up to a solid crescendo. Then the Beatles appeared escorted by twelve policemen. The screaming became ear-splitting and together with the thousands of flashbulbs popping it was as if a thunder-storm had broken out.

The Beatles could hardly be heard over the frenzy, but that didn't seem to matter to the ecstatic fans. The noise was so deafening that the boys couldn't even hear themselves play. They had to use sign language, even when Paul and George were singing together into the same microphone. But it was not only the crowd noise they had to contend with. The acoustics of the arena produced a semi-echo that would have enhanced the music if the crowd had been quiet. Instead it enhanced the din! Far from discouraging the Beatles, all the noise and excitement made them play and sing marvellously; they triumphed over the odds and made it a fantastic occasion.

At the end of their performance the Beatles dropped their instruments and bolted up one of the aisles to the dressing room, surrounded and protected by a flying wedge of police. As the only entrance to the dressing room was through the men's toilet, this stopped the girls from following them. Backstage the boys were soaking wet, sweat pouring off them.

The Beatles were exhilarated by the reception from the Washington kids. A delirious Ringo said ". . . they could have ripped me apart and I couldn't have cared less. What an audience! I could have played for them all night." All the boys felt the same way – I had never heard them speak so highly of an audience.

Back at the hotel the boys took a shower, charged into their 'Sunday Best' and prepared themselves for the ball at the British Embassy. I was so exhausted that I declined the invitation, preferring to relax in the huge bath in my hotel suite. Afterwards, judging from what I heard from the boys, I was the cleverest of the lot. They came back looking almost like vagrants, their clothes messed up and a chunk of Ringo's hair missing. They were all quite upset. Apparently, the diplomats and their families behaved as if the Beatles were a freak show for their amusement.

When I went to wake the Beatles the next morning, they were already up and dressed and raring to leave Washington. The Embassy incident had left a bad taste in their mouths. After a good breakfast I thanked my new-found compatriot, the assistant manager, for all his help, and we departed for the railway station, – on time for a change.

During the return journey to New York, the train driver purposely slowed down when we passed through the stations along the route as they were all packed with waving and cheering kids. When the boys realised what was happening they went over to the windows and waved to the fans, overwhelmed by the happy welcome. The Beatles became so choked they couldn't speak. I wish I could have captured their emotions with my camera, but there were special moments like this when I didn't take pictures. I never wanted to invade their privacy, which was one of the reasons I rarely used a flash. I often took photos with the camera under my arm in order not to intimidate the boys.

That same evening the Beatles were set to perform two concerts at the prestigious Carnegie Hall in New York. I was the last from the entourage to leave the hotel for the concerts, but instead of going in straightaway I decided to photograph the crowds. By the time I finished it was too late for me to get in – the police had cordoned off the hall. I wandered around taking pictures until I heard a different kind of Beatle chanting. This was not the distinctive friendly shouts of fans, but the noise of the anti-Beatle brigade and their 'Stamp Out The Beatles' campaign. Crowds of anti-Beatle boys were holding up banners and jumping around and yelling, congregating near a big brightly-lit delicatessen window display, against which I was able to take a picture of them without flash.

The Beatles later told me I didn't miss anything at Carnegie Hall. "It was like a big church hall," Ringo said.

WASHINGTON DC

PAGE 82
Top: *On the train from New York to Washington the boys tended to spread themselves out, making it difficult for photographers after shots of the Fab Four together. I asked them to sit closer and they kindly did so, consuming several cokes and cigarettes in the process.* **Bottom:** *The snow-covered American landscape was a revelation. The Beatles had so far experienced only the skyscrapers of New York. Now they stared, fascinated at the complete contrast of wooden shacks and scrap-yards lining the railroad tracks.*

PAGE 83
Top: *A press photographer reels back in disbelief as Ringo turns the tables on him.* **Bottom left:** *Paul's turn with a camera.*

PAGE 84
Fed up with Beatlemania saturating the radio waves, Ringo sat by himself and concentrated on his photography. He was particularly interested in the snow-covered wooden houses with typical American-style porches along the route.

PAGE 85
Top: *One of Ringo's own shots. The poorest wooden shacks were made picturesque by the blanket of snow.* **Bottom:** *The conductor in charge of the Beatles' coach became good friends with Ringo. Here he is explaining the route and the timetables.*

PAGE 86
Top: *With this shot I captured the look of the coach lengthwise. You can see the luxurious seats which swivelled and reclined and helped make the trip comfortable.* **Bottom:** *American newspapers and magazines with their unfamiliar advertisements intrigued the boys, but their attention was easily distracted.*

PAGE 87
Top: *George Martin also became engrossed in the scenery.* **Bottom left:** *Armed with one of my cameras, Ringo looms over Paul.* **Bottom right:** *George Martin being interviewed by Al Aronowitz from* The Saturday Evening Post.

PAGE 88
Top: *The only teenagers allowed on the platform at Washington's Union Station were the lucky few employed by WWDC to hold up the radio station's welcoming banner. The fans were left screaming outside the station gates.* **Bottom:** *The platform where we disembarked was very narrow. I walked backwards through the crush of police, press and photographers in order to get this picture.*

PAGE 89
The press conference in the Coliseum sports arena. You can see the rows of empty wooden seats and the rather dim house lighting. It was an exciting occasion, but rather cold.

PAGE 90
Top left: *Outside the Coliseum stadium. This was the very first Beatles' live concert in America. Naturally, it was sold out.* **Top right:** *At this time, just before the concert, the stage was empty except for the boys' equipment which had been set up beforehand by Neil Aspinall and Mal Evans. Special security police guarded the stage from over-enthusiastic fans.* **Bottom:** *One of the most exciting concerts so far. The group played on the boxing ring itself, and Ringo's drum-kit was on a special revolving platform, though it eventually had to be stopped to keep Ringo from feeling sick.*

PAGE 91
Top left: *John ecstatic, completely in his element.* **Top right:** *Paul, just as happy and even more sweaty.* **Bottom left:** *George was the coolest member of the squad.* **Bottom right:** *For Ringo, this particular show stood out. Backstage he was full of enthusiasm for the Washington fans.*

PAGE 92
Top: *Lennon and McCartney singing together. The overwhelming atmosphere at the Coliseum made them work together more closely than I'd ever seen before. They needed to use the same microphone in order to synchronise their vocals and harmonies; lip-reading was compulsory in the tremendous din.* **Bottom:** *After the show, the gear was ready to go and the thousands of jelly beans had to be swept up.*

PAGE 93
On the way back to Union Station, we all packed into two cars. I begged our driver to stop for a couple of minutes when I saw the Capital building.

PAGE 94
Top: *At the rear of the specially added railroad coach was an observation platform which had not been opened on the way down to Washington. On the return journey the authorities allowed us to use it, with Ringo especially making good use of the facility for photographic purposes.* **Bottom left:** *The ice-cold weather brought masses of steam from the train. This was the atmospheric scene from the observation platform as we pulled away from the station.* **Bottom right:** *Ringo waits on the observation platform with my cinecamera, waiting for something to film, while George peeps at him from inside, just about to photograph Ringo the cameraman.*

PAGE 95
Top: *A critical assessment of the highly successful Coliseum concert – and the Embassy fiasco. John and George Martin also discuss the concert that night at New York's Carnegie Hall.* **Bottom:** *These girls followed the boys from New York to Washington in the hope of meeting them, finally tracking down their idols on the train back to New York.*

PAGE 96
Top: *Ringo, King Of The Railroad.* **Bottom left:** *Filming in the coach.* **Bottom right:** *George climbed up to the luggage rack for a little snooze, but as usual he was pestered by photographers and fellow Beatles.*

PAGE 97
Top: *A pyramid of Beatles. This time it was Paul's turn to wear my Astrakhan hat.* **Bottom:** *Gringo.*

PAGE 98
Top: *Ringo looking for something, anything, to photograph.* **Bottom:** *Refreshments for George, John and a disguised Cynthia. By this time it was already dark outside.*

PAGE 99
Top: *It was so cold that the windows were frozen even on the inside.* **Bottom:** *As the train gets nearer to New York, George sees some tall buildings and begins to take more pictures.*

PAGE 100
Top: *Weary, the Fab Four try to relax. John still clutches his BEA(tles) flight bag.* **Bottom:** *At the last stop, a policeman comes into their coach and the boys oblige with autographs.*

PAGE 101
Top: *The exterior of New York's prestigious Carnegie Hall, where both Beatles concerts were completely sold out.* **Bottom:** *The Stamp Out The Beatles brigade, a small but noisy minority.*

WASHINGTON DC

81

82

WASHINGTON DC

WASHINGTON DC

85

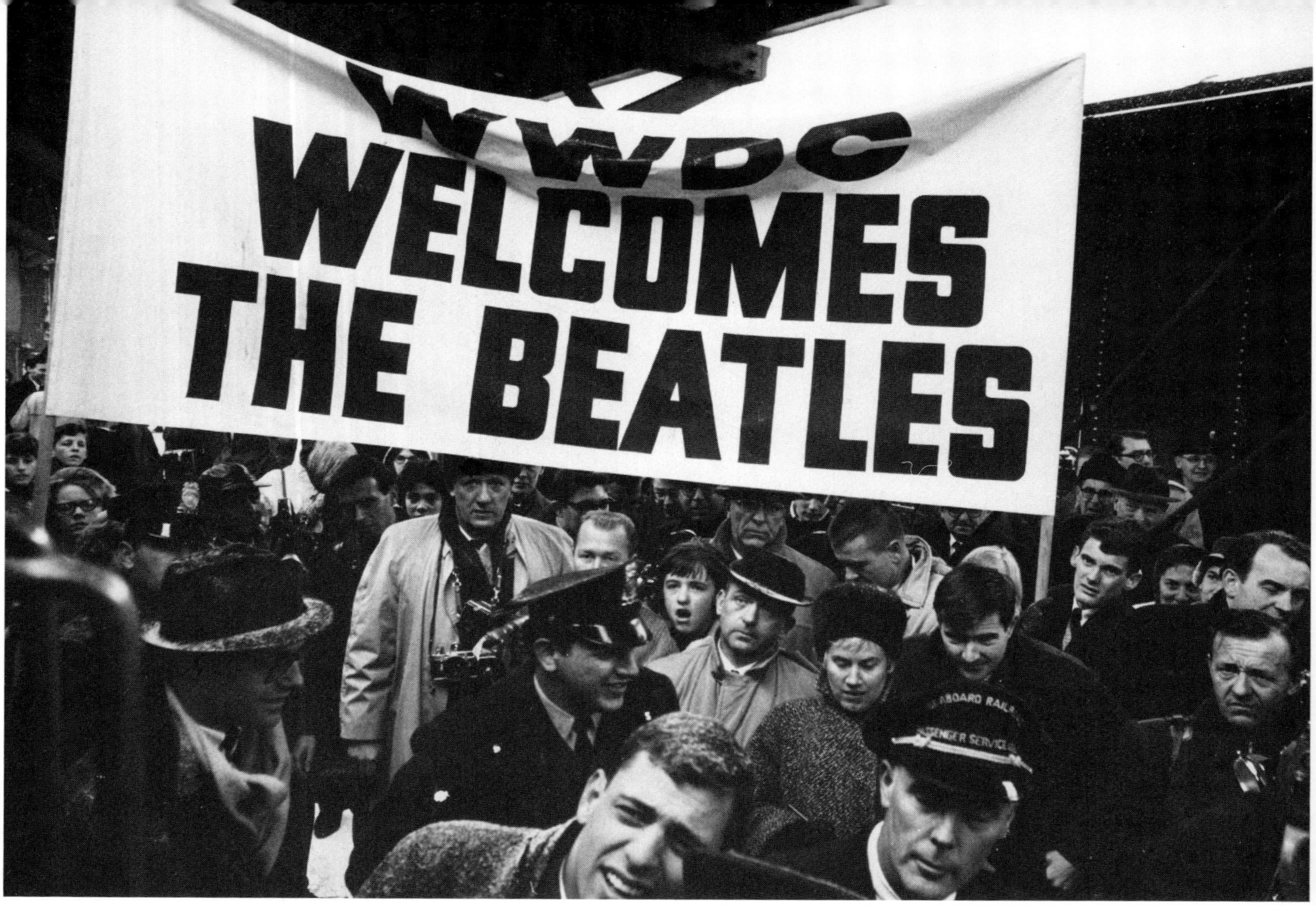
WWDC
WELCOMES
THE BEATLES

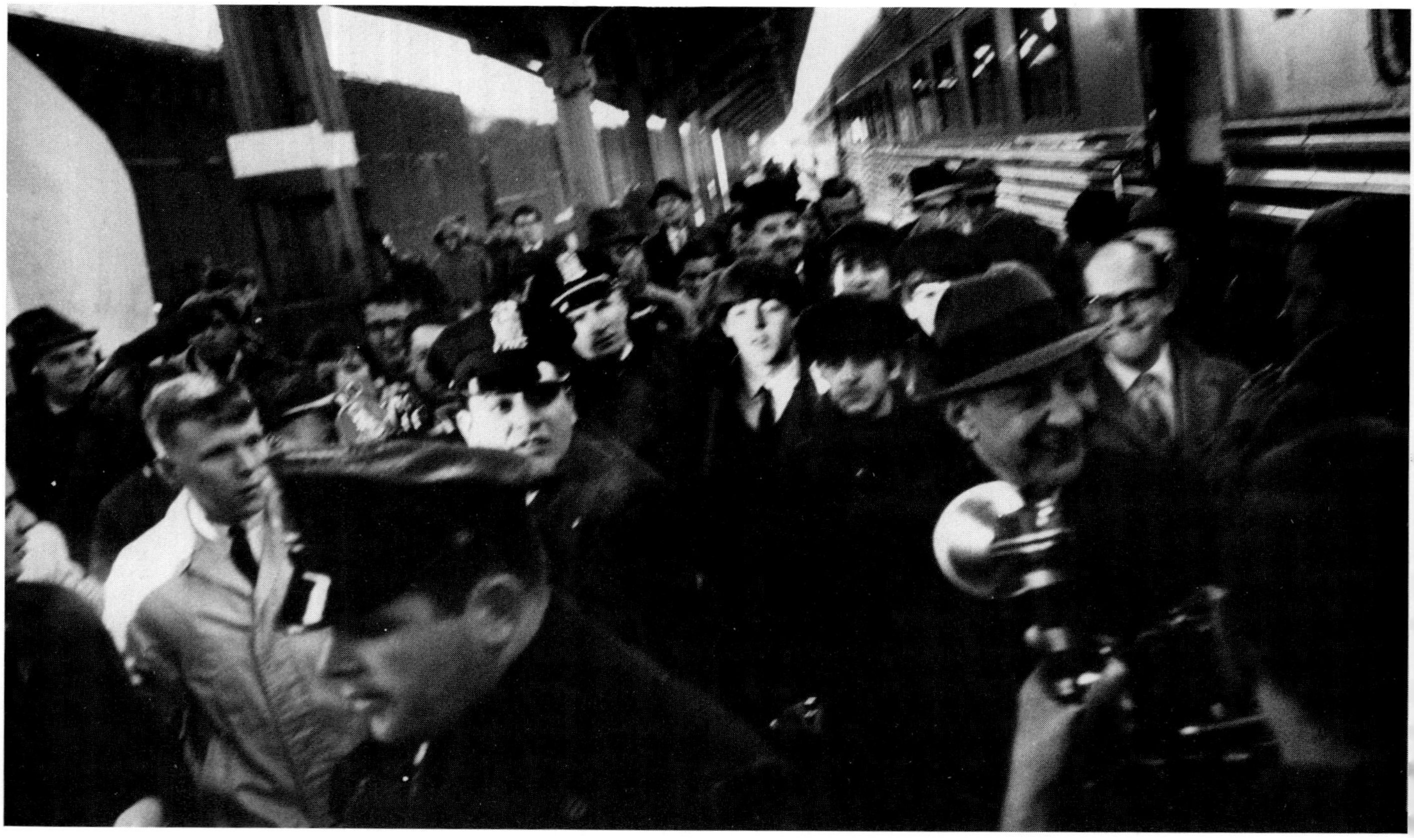

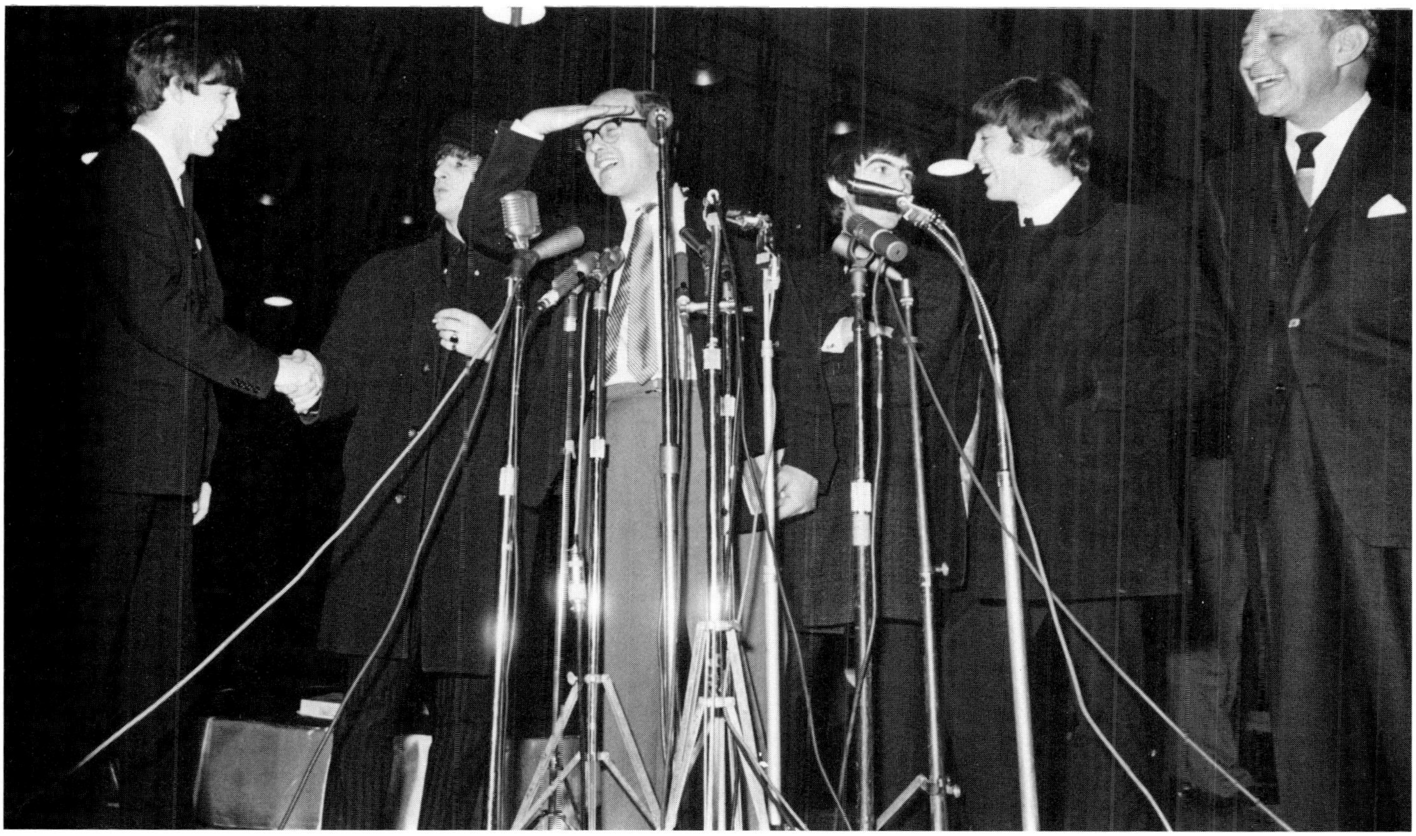

WASHINGTON DC

COLISEUM
TUES NITE FEB 11 830 PM
THE BEATLES
SOLD OUT
COLISEUM
TUES NITE FEB 11 830 PM
THE BEATLES
SOLD OUT

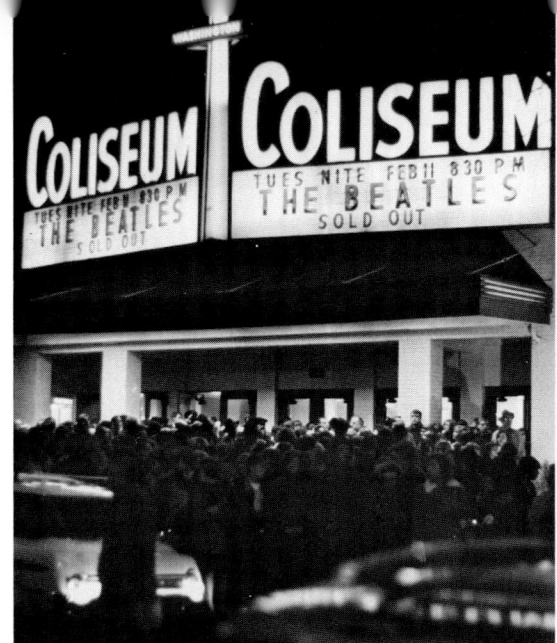

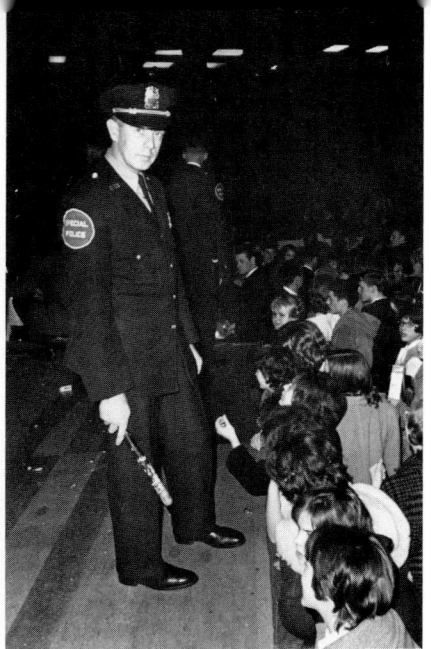

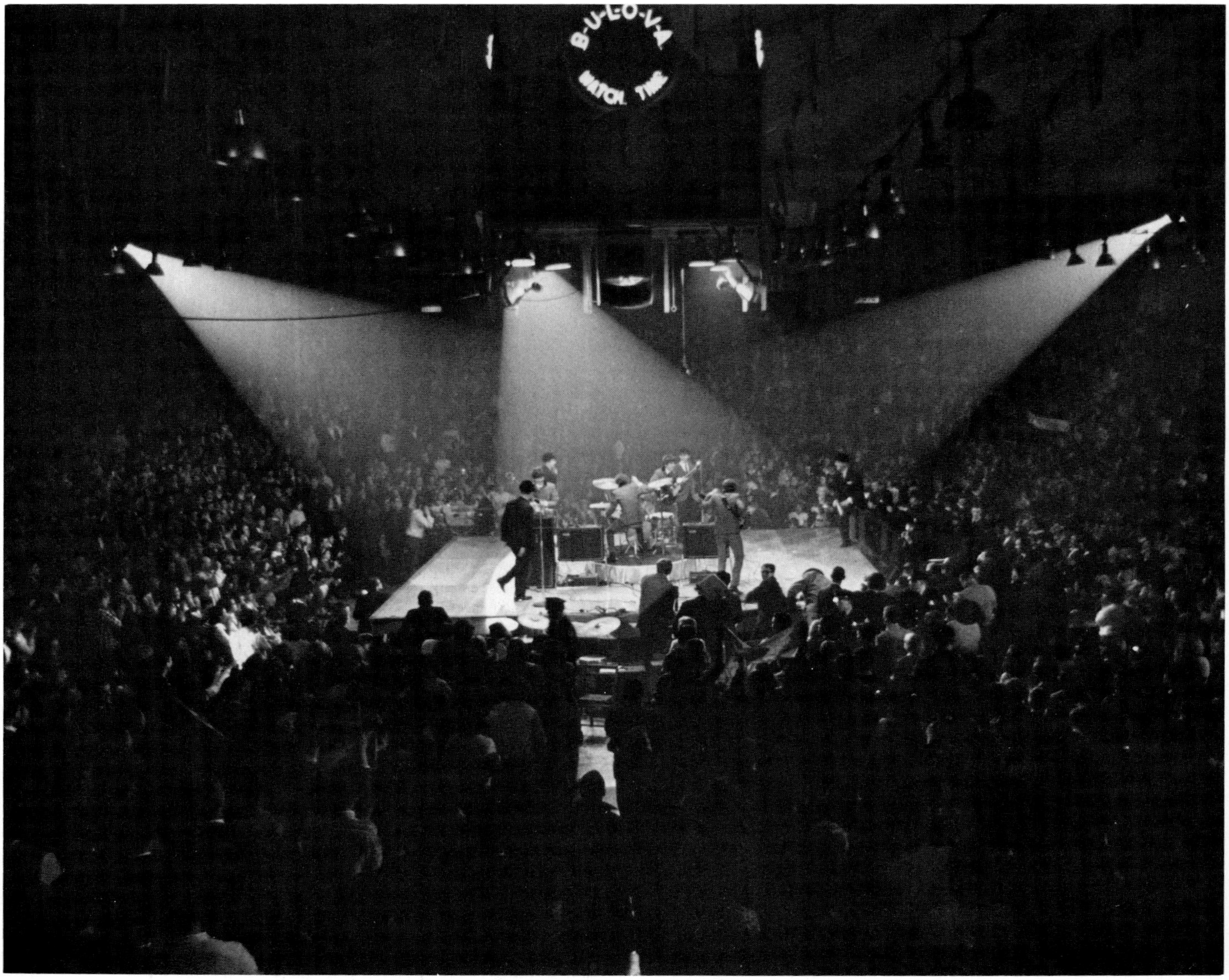
B-U-L-O-V-A
WATCH TIME

WASHINGTON DC

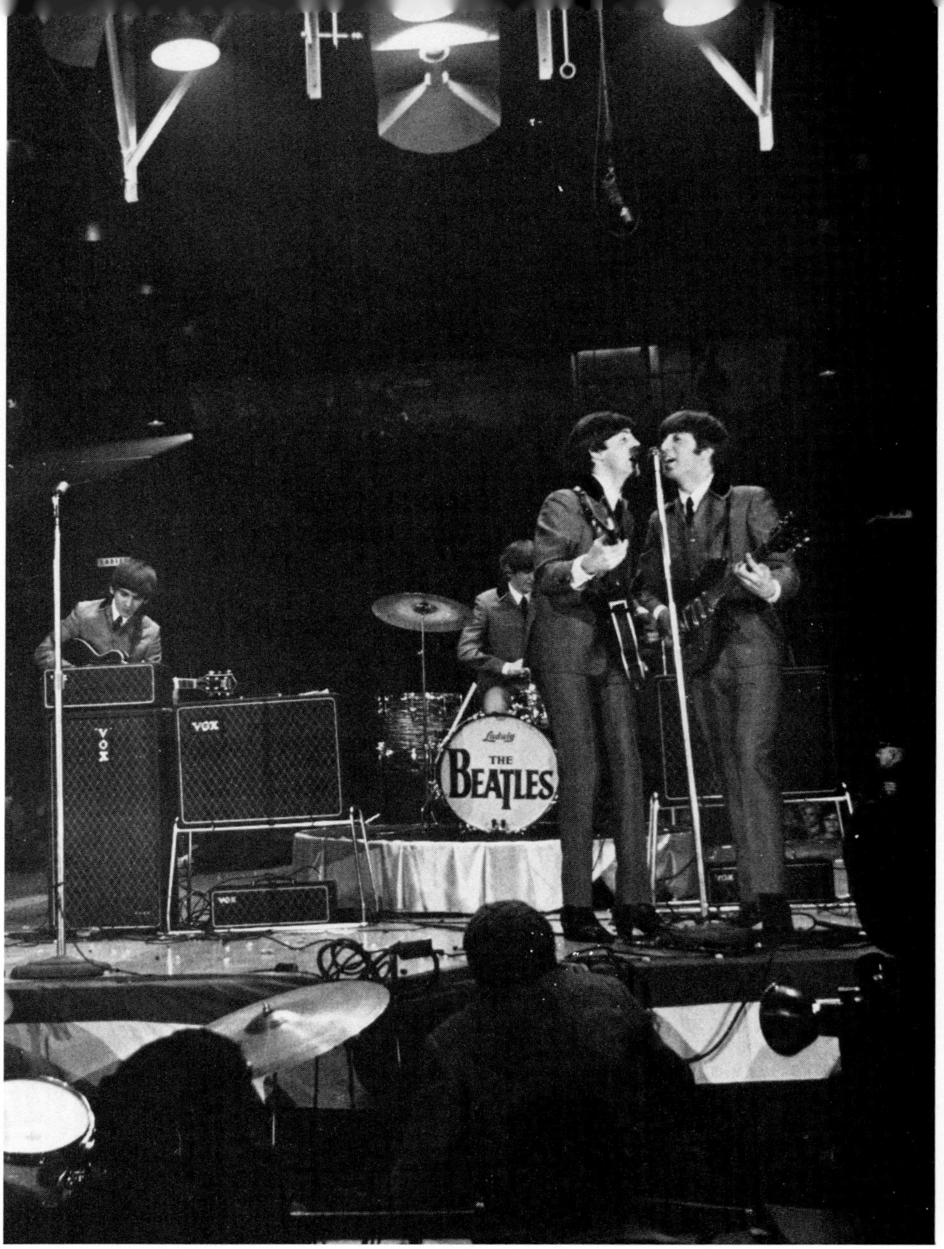
VOX
VOX
VOX
Ludwig
THE
BEATLES

Ludwig
THE
BEATLES

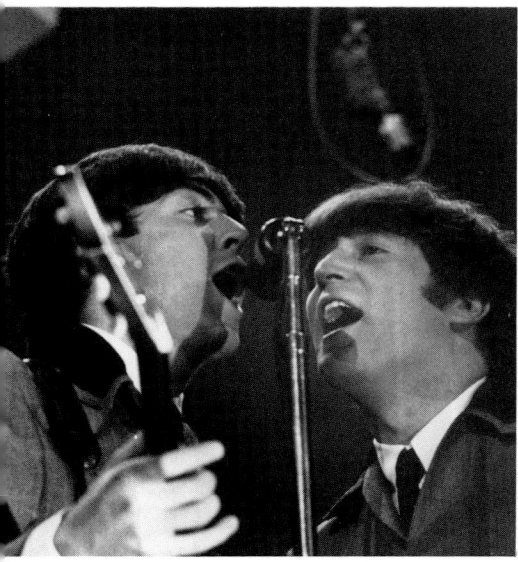

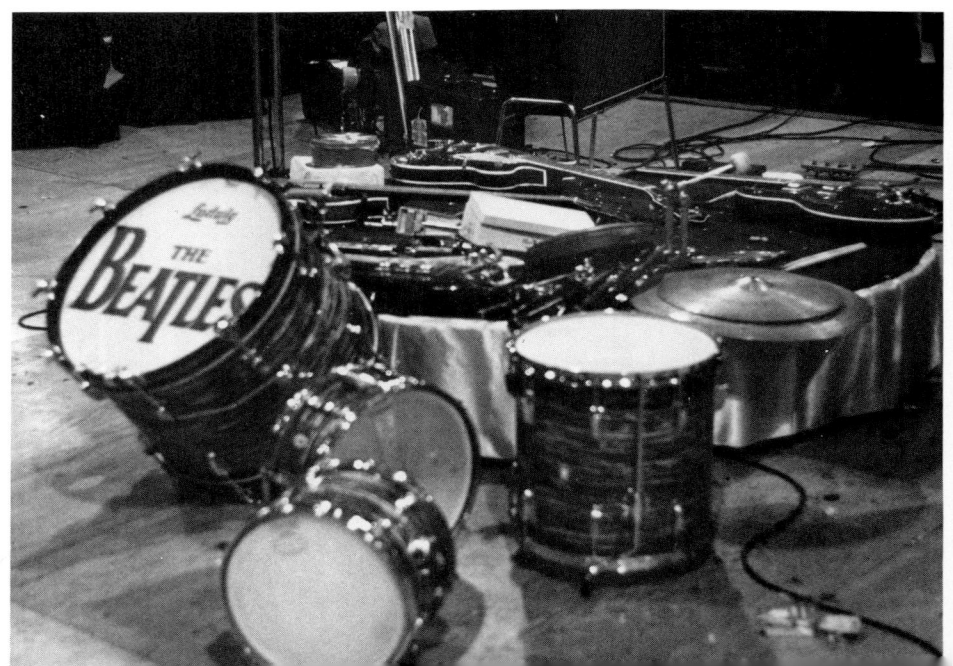

WASHINGTON DC

WASHINGTON DC

WASHINGTON DC

WASHINGTON DC

98

WASHINGTON DC

WASHINGTON DC

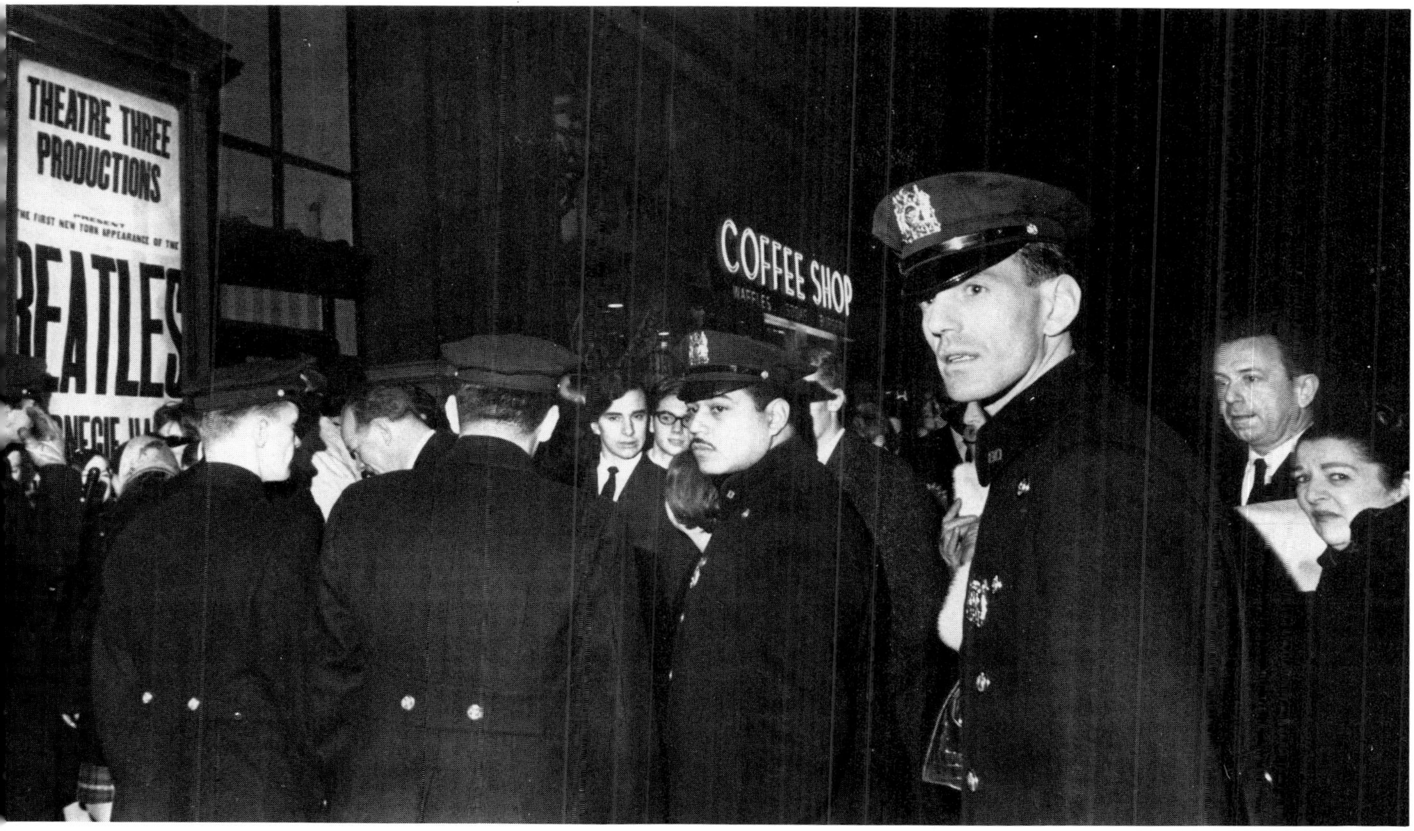
THEATRE THREE
PRODUCTIONS
COFFEE SHOP

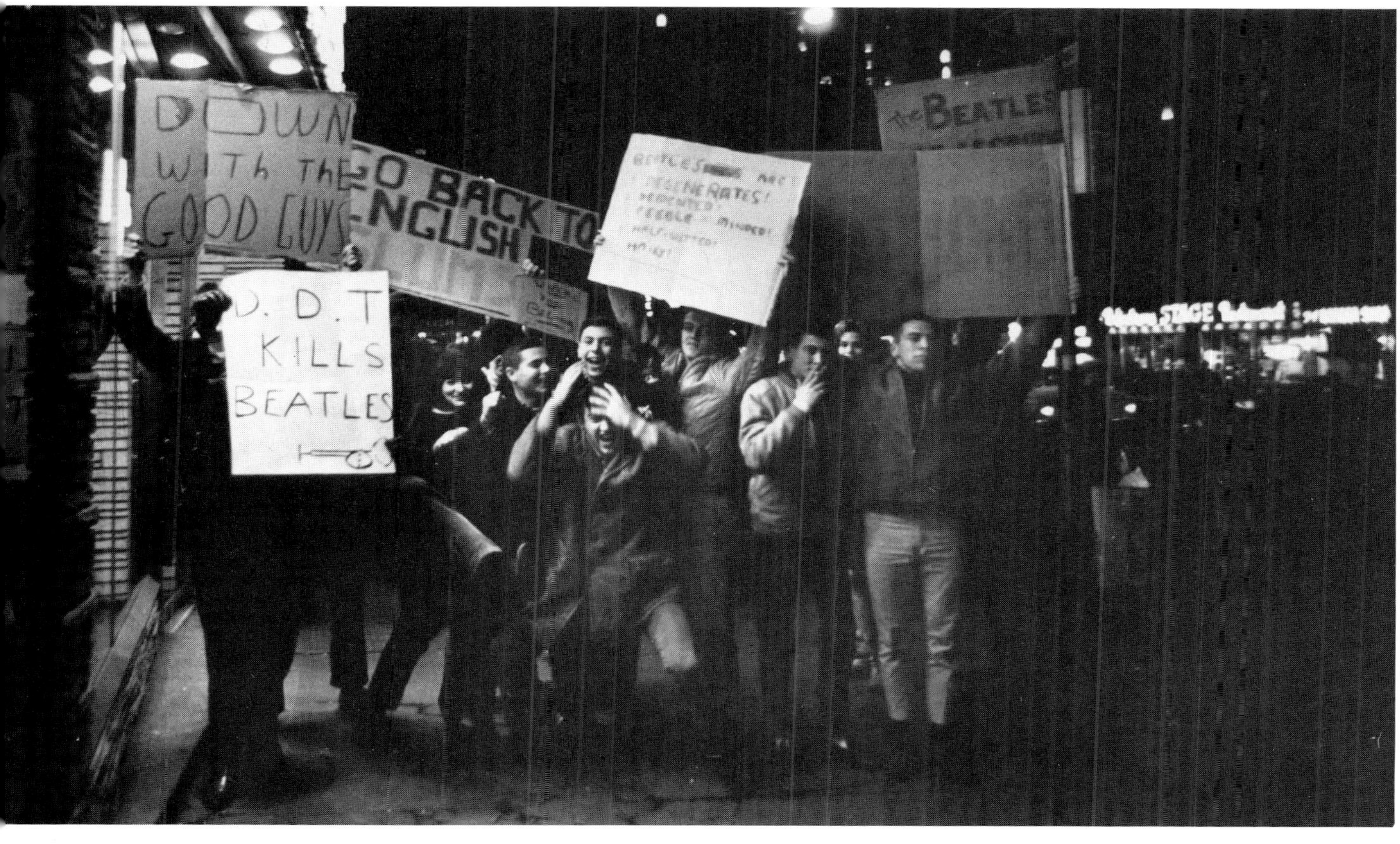
D. D. T
KILLS
BEATLES
GO BACK TO

MIAMI

The Beatles still didn't trust American airlines, and on the flight to Miami our pilot made them even worse by walking into the passenger area wearing a Beatle wig. Nevertheless they were glad to get away from New York's bitter cold, and were looking forward to sunbathing in Florida.

We landed at Miami and the minute the plane doors opened we were hit by a heatwave. Everyone was still wearing their winter clothing and it was so hot we had difficulty breathing. The noise from the plane was incredible, – almost as loud as the noise from the crowds! Miami airport wasn't so big in those days, but a huge welcoming committee turned out, including several beauty queens, all of whom had orders to kiss the Beatles.

Most of the fans had arrived in their own cars, so unlike New York we couldn't lose them when we left the airport. Hundreds of them followed and tried to overtake us, racing alongside to catch a glimpse of the Beatles. Looking back it seems funny, but at the time it was frightening how close they got. Police motorcycles escorted our convoy to the Deauville Hotel where we had to fight our way through the fans in the forecourt.

The Deauville foyer was so packed that the Beatles were rushed straight up to their own suites to book in. Minutes later the media were falling over themselves for interviews.

After settling into the hotel, the pressure from the local press became so overpowering that the Beatles could no longer handle being continuously bothered with interviews in their suites, so Brian Sommerville held a press conference on the second day in the hotel's Mau Mau club. That place sticks in my memory mainly because it was so gloomy and uninviting. Most photographers had to use flash and not many good pictures were taken. I stuck to my own technique of not using flash, and fortunately, it worked.

So great was the responsibility of protecting the Beatles that the Miami Police Department specially assigned Sergeant Buddy Dresner to take care of their security. He was allocated over twenty policemen to help him. The protection of the Beatles was literally a 24 hour-a-day job and Dresner was forced to temporarily abandon his family and stay with them at the Deauville. He devised a secret lapel badge, set up booby traps for invading fans, and arranged ingenious means of escape from the hotel. His job was difficult, not only because of the fans but because the Beatles themselves often felt like going out and looking for fun during their week in Miami. Even the simplest excursion required planning for security. The Beatles were fast becoming used to being virtual hotel prisoners.

The Beatles certainly brought out the crazy side of many people. At the Deauville the adults were worse than the kids; they all wanted a slice of the Beatles. I remember seeing road manager Mal Evans pinned to the wall by some guests, four women and a man, demanding to know if he were a Beatle. Foolishly, he said yes, and that was it. They wouldn't let him go until he had signed dozens of autographs and answered all their questions, – and he looked nothing like any of the Beatles! All sorts of people would stop me in the lobby and offer hundreds of dollars for a ticket to see the next Beatles appearance on the Sullivan Show, due to be broadcast from the Deauville's Napoleon Rooms. Women would parade by the Olympic-size pool wearing fur coats in the sweltering weather, just to show off that fact that they had a fur.

I got a real shock in the hotel restaurant. The food was magnificent, really fabulous, but the portions were criminal. One meal would have fed three people. All the waiters were Cuban refugees and when they cleared the tables with the heaps of left-overs they were very careful taking the food off the plates; it would no doubt be going home to their refugee families. The Beatles couldn't go near the restaurant; they would have been torn to pieces.

The hotel management were soon sympathetic to the Beatles' problems with privacy and it was arranged for them to spend some of their days at a private villa owned by a local millionaire, Bernie Castro. The actual villa once owned by the infamous gangster Al Capone was just a few doors away.

The first day the Beatles spent at the villa was the day the photo session for *Life* magazine was scheduled. The boys were driven from Castro's villa to another nearby in their swimming trunks. It was a similar villa except with a much nicer pool. The back of the garden faced the sea instead of one of the canals. The boys were puzzled when they saw the *Life* photographer's flash umbrella. "Why does he need flash in this sun?" they asked. The boys were to be photographed in the pool and the flash was necessary to stop their faces being in shadow from the fierce mid-day sun which reflected off the water and shone down onto their heads. It should only have taken a few minutes for the shots to be taken, but it took half an hour. This was mostly due to the fact that the photographer had to work to a pre-arranged layout; the boys' heads all had to be positioned in a certain place in the water. The film was needed in New York that same day, and in the picture that was finally used, John's eyes are shut.

During their days at the villa the boys learned various new skills. Sgt. Dresner taught them how to fish, though at first they didn't like handling live bait or taking the fish off the hooks. They all tried hard at fishing. George was the most successful, hooking a catch almost every time he cast his line.

The food at the villa was glorious. There was a 'houseboy' on the staff, a black man who was from the Bahamas and terribly proud of being British. He was very nice to us as we were fellow-Britishers, and put together fantastic barbecues. There was so much food and drink it was unbelievable. All the Beatles indulged in the feasting, but Ringo especially enjoyed himself. He could nearly always be found by the table.

One day the Beatles visited the home of Sgt. Dresner and had dinner with his family. It was a simple down-to-earth occasion, perhaps the only one during the whole of their American trip. The boys found it very relaxing to be amongst ordinary people again. For them, it was like being with their own families. The day was not only relaxing, but somewhat educational because this was a real American family with all the little differences. It gave them their first insight into the way of life of ordinary Americans.

George loved driving and managed to hire himself an open-top MGB sports car, which wasn't an easy car to hire in Florida. He was quite thrilled, but when he showed Brian Epstein the bright red sports car Brian was like a jealous kid saying, "I want a car too!" So

Brian hired himself an identical MGB, though he had to settle for beige. They kept them both parked side-by-side at the hotel.

George would go driving for hours at a time and I used to try to photograph him in the car, but despite spending over $80 on taxis I could rarely catch him. He was usually accompanied by a policeman, but one day he motored off with Del Shannon who was then working in Miami and offered to show George the local countryside between engagements.

The first rehearsals for the Ed Sullivan Show were nothing like New York. It was so hot the Beatles had to rehearse in a cool storage room adjacent to the hotel pool. The management emptied the room to make way for the boys and their equipment. The boys would come straight out of the pool and rehearse in their swimming trunks.

The dress rehearsal was held in the Napoleon Rooms where the show itself would be televised. There was a huge audience and the Beatles treated it like a real concert, giving their all and delighting everyone.

But the TV show itself was something very special. Five thousand people were jammed inside, – screaming, weeping and fainting even before the Beatles began to play. There was so much excitement and electricity generated, such a tremendous atmosphere, that the hotel manager said it even overshadowed Judy Garland's comeback in the same room. It was estimated that over 75 million people watched the Ed Sullivan show that evening, and the boys performed magnificently.

After the show a small dinner party was thrown for the Beatles, the other acts on the show, including Mitzi Gaynor, and all the backroom boys. Everybody had a good time and there were no hassles with fans. The TV technicians from the Ed Sullivan Show said the Beatles were the most friendly and cooperative performers they'd ever worked with.

Following the Sullivan show the Beatles had several days to relax. At the villa they met a young man willing to teach them water ski-ing. Unfortunately for me, this led to an eventual rift with John. Although my basic expenses for the American trip were paid by CBS-TV, as mentioned earlier, I needed to supplement my expenses by taking pictures for magazines and newspapers back home. One magazine later printed a picture of mine of John water ski-ing in which his hair was, quite naturally, blown back by the wind. When John saw the picture he was livid. He was terribly vain about his hair and insisted it be pictured swept forward covering his forehead. He carried on that feud with me for a long, long time. Poor John also had a nasty mishap when he was first learning to water ski. While practising with the skis in the villa pool, he fell and hurt his back quite badly, so perhaps this made my picture all the more annoying to him.

Inside the hotel were a number of shops, one of them a hairdressing salon. Jerry Liston, wife of world heavyweight boxing champion Sonny Liston, worked there, and Liston himself used to spend a lot of time just sitting outside the shop. He was a huge man and not very pretty, and I'm sure he must have frightened several customers away. He didn't like the Beatles and wasn't interested when I suggested photographing them with him. The boys were too scared to go down and meet him; they'd just peep around the corner. He was scheduled to fight Cassius Clay for the championship, and that fight was the big news story from Miami. As luck would have it, the Beatles did meet Cassius Clay and some terrific pictures were taken of them together.

The meeting was suggested by fight promoter Harold Conrad, who realized the publicity value in getting Clay and the Beatles together, but unfortunately Brian Epstein said no to the idea. However, at a party after the Sullivan Show the Beatles were introduced to Conrad by Sullivan. John was particularly impressed by Clay, and all the Beatles favoured him to win. Conrad invited them to watch Clay work out and they all went haywire and jumped at the chance. Conrad said "OK, but don't tell Brian." "Don't worry, John said, "we'll handle him." The next morning we were picked up by limousines and taken to the gym.

Although this was a meeting of the giants, the Beatles didn't mind Clay showing off at their expense. They didn't have much choice! He was a wonderful self-publicist and choreographed all the 'fight' pictures between him and the boys. When it came to witty one-liners, though, the Beatles were just as quick as Clay. It was a very happy occasion. I was laughing so much I had trouble taking pictures. At the end of the work-out Clay conceded that the Beatles were the greatest but insisted he was still the prettiest.

MIAMI

PAGE 106
Top: *The welcoming beauties at Miami airport wore bathing costumes in the intense heat, with sashes reading: 'WQAM Welcomes The Beatles To Miami'.* **Bottom:** *As the Beatles leave the airport and the welcoming committee disbands, down come the sandwich boards and placards, all provided by WQAM, Miami's major pop radio station.*

PAGE 107
Top: *I took a taxi from Miami airport to the Deauville Hotel. The entire Beatles convoy was escorted by police motorcycles, and I had a wonderful, though worrying view of the fans' cars racing alongside to catch a glimpse of the boys.* **Centre:** *At night, almost every window in the Deauville Hotel was a different colour and it made a beautiful colour shot. Still, I couldn't resist including this photo in black-and-white.* **Bottom:** *The Mau Mau Club, the suitably dark nightspot at the hotel where the improvised press reception was held. It was too dark for good pictures, but all the local press were in attendance.*

PAGE 108
Top: *Brian joins the 'Stamp Out The Beatles' brigade, watched by an amused Maurice Kinn, owner of the London* New Musical Express. **Top:** *Ringo in his bedroom at the Deauville Hotel, admiring himself in one of my Beatles sweat-shirts before going down to the pool. Note the copy of* Cashbox *and the chocolate box on the table.* **Bottom:** *Road manager Neil Aspinall (in bed on the phone) and PR Brian Sommerville hard at work straight after breakfast, preparing the day's busy schedule.*

PAGE 109
Bottom: *Among the visitors to the Beatles at the Deauville was Del Shannon, who knew the boys from his tours of the UK. Del even had a small American hit in 1963 with a cover version of 'From Me To You.'*

PAGE 110
The view from Paul's bedroom at the Deauville overlooking the beach. The fans couldn't shout up to the Beatles over the noise of the sea, so they wrote messages in the sand using stones, driftwood, and palm fronds. Unfortunately, the frequent tides kept washing away their lovingly constructed messages.

PAGE 111
Paul after a good swim.

PAGE 112
Photographer John Loengard lines up the Beatles for the exact layout needed for the cover of Life *magazine.* **Bottom:** *Gingerly taking their first steps into the unheated pool. It was a hot day with bright sun, but the pool was still cold. Note the flash umbrella.*

PAGE 113
Top: *A shot similar to the one used on the* Life *cover.* **Bottom:** *Getting accustomed to the cold water. You can see* Life *photographer John Loengard at the poolside.*

PAGE 114
Top: *With the family who owned the villa.* **Bottom:** *Relaxing at the villa where the* Life *session was shot. By this time John had his 'Beatle boots' back on.*

PAGE 115
Top left: *John showing off his prowess with a so-called swallow dive.* **Bottom:** *John practising with his water-skis at the villa pool where he fell and hurt his back. His instructor is in the pool.*

PAGES 116 & 117
These hats worn by John and Paul were the only pieces of merchandising that I remember which didn't get the Beatles' own approval for a license. They only wore them for these photographs. Looking back I now realise why they didn't like the hats – they covered their hair!

PAGE 118
At the villa owned by Bernie Castro. **Bottom:** *The Beatles were camera crazy. Here they are hunting for pictures after rummaging through my bag and each finding themselves a camera. They'd photograph anything from feet upwards.*

PAGE 119
Top: *Reading the first reports from the press conference the previous afternoon in the local Miami paper. It was a good write-up but they always read their own reviews with thoughtfulness, – thus the serious expressions.* **Bottom:** *Brian and John have a more relaxed chat.*

PAGES 120 & 121
Enjoying a few rare moments of peace and quiet. **Page 120, Top:** *John and Cynthia.*

PAGE 122
Ringo at the table, spoiled for choice.

PAGE 123
Portrait of Paul.

PAGE 124
Top: *Ringo fell into the canal alongside the villa and all his dollar bills had to be dried out in the sun. Here he is with Neil Aspinall unpeeling them from each other. Luckily he didn't have all his money on him at the time!*

PAGE 125
A candid portrait of George and Ringo.

PAGES 126 & 127
Eating with the family who owned the villa. **Page 127, Bottom left:** *Gossiping with neighbours over the garden fence.*

PAGES 128 & 129
George learns how to fish under the experienced eye of Sgt. Buddy Dresner. The Miami canals were murky but alive with fish, and after the boys' initial reluctance to handle live bait and unhook their squirming catches, they soon warmed to the sport.

PAGES 130 & 131
The Beatles were quick learners; they found fishing to be an ideal relaxation. Once they'd mastered the rudiments of fishing, the boys took their tackle on to small boats and began fishing in the canals and the sea.

PAGES 132 & 133
Top: *After searching for George for hours and hours in a taxi, I eventually found Brian Epstein and George Martin sightseeing in Brian's hired MGB.* **Page 132, Bottom:** *The only photo I took of George in his bright red hired MGB. It was the first time he had been able to afford to hire a car, and even then it was illegal because he was under-age; he was still two weeks away from his 21st birthday.*

PAGE 134
Paul was always like a Pied Piper to children, and the Dresner kids were no exception. Paul spent most of his time on the visit reading to the children and showing them photos from my first book of Beatle pictures which was published in 1963. He was a complete slave to them.

MIAMI

PAGE 135
Visiting the home of Sgt. Buddy Dresner. The policeman's family cooked a marvellous roast beef dinner for everyone, including the ever-present Murray the K.

PAGE 136
Even in the sea the Beatles couldn't escape from their admirers, but sometimes fans could be fun. Here they are frolicking with some girls from Miami Beach High School who were working as part-time models at a car show. **Bottom right:** Ringo with fans Barbara Turchin and Carol Olesky; he later dated Barbara, taking her to a drive-in movie. When the Beatles left Miami, as a parting gift Ringo gave her . . . a ring.

PAGE 137
Top: Ringo gives a rudimentary lesson on his drum kit to a lady member of the CBS-TV technical staff. **Bottom:** Ringo and Paul sign autographs.

PAGES 138 & 139
This was the 'cool room' next to the Deauville swimming pool where the Beatles rehearsed for the Sullivan Show. It was ideal for them because they could come straight in from the pool, pick up their instruments and get to work – still in their swimming trunks.

PAGE 140
This was taken at the first rehearsal in the Deauville's Napoleon Rooms, where the Ed Sullivan Show was later to be televised. Lack of space meant that the boys' make-up was done in front of all and sundry at the Napoleon Rooms. Here's John receiving a few finishing touches.

PAGE 141
Bottom: John looks very proud as the Beatles are presented with an honorary college fraternity plaque from two gentleman scholars during the Sullivan show dress rehearsals.

PAGE 142
Top: The big night – the Beatles' second live appearance on the Ed Sullivan Show, with Ringo looking suitably unimpressed as Ed tells the frenzied audience to calm down. **Bottom left:** The late Ed Sullivan himself, America's foremost master of ceremonies and the man who first presented both Elvis Presley and the Beatles to the people of America. **Bottom right:** Singing to America. That evening Sullivan's ratings exceeded even the first Beatles appearance on his show.

PAGE 143
Top: By this time it was not only the kids who had fallen for the Beatles, the adults loved them too. But from both adults and kids the reaction was usually the same – complete fascination. **Bottom left:** A contented George Martin watching rehearsals. **Bottom right:** I took this shot in one of the mirrors on the walls of the Deauville's Napoleon Rooms. That way I could capture the audience, the TV cameras and the boys themselves onstage.

PAGE 144
Fans at the Deauville during the show.

PAGE 145
Top: Guests at the party after the show included comedian Don Rickles (seated) and the owner of the Flamingo Hotel, Las Vegas, whose hat seems a little too small for George's head. **Bottom left:** The Beatles hadn't forgotten their French salutes! **Bottom right:** Paul with actress/singer/dancer Mitzi Gaynor who appeared with them on the show.

PAGES 146 & 147
The Beatles loved water. Here they are water-skiing and larking about in boats on the Miami canals.

PAGE 148
Brian peruses the concert review.

PAGE 149
Captain John.

PAGES 150 & 151
A real American holiday, boating in style.

PAGES 152 & 153
This was Cassius Clay's easiest victory. With his pretty face and big mouth he won the championship against Liverpool's own Fab Four. The exchange of quick wit kept me laughing so hard I could hardly hold my camera steady.

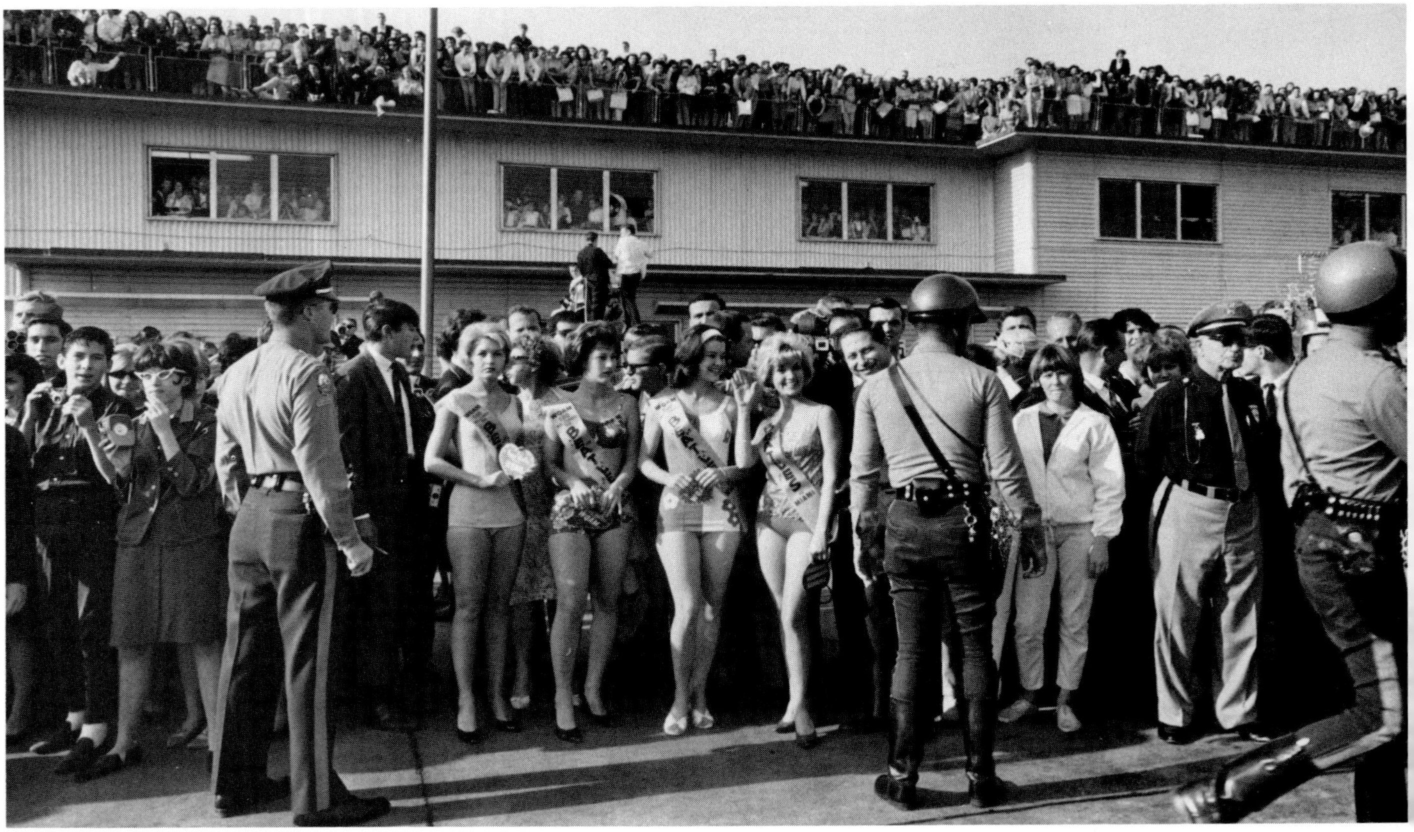

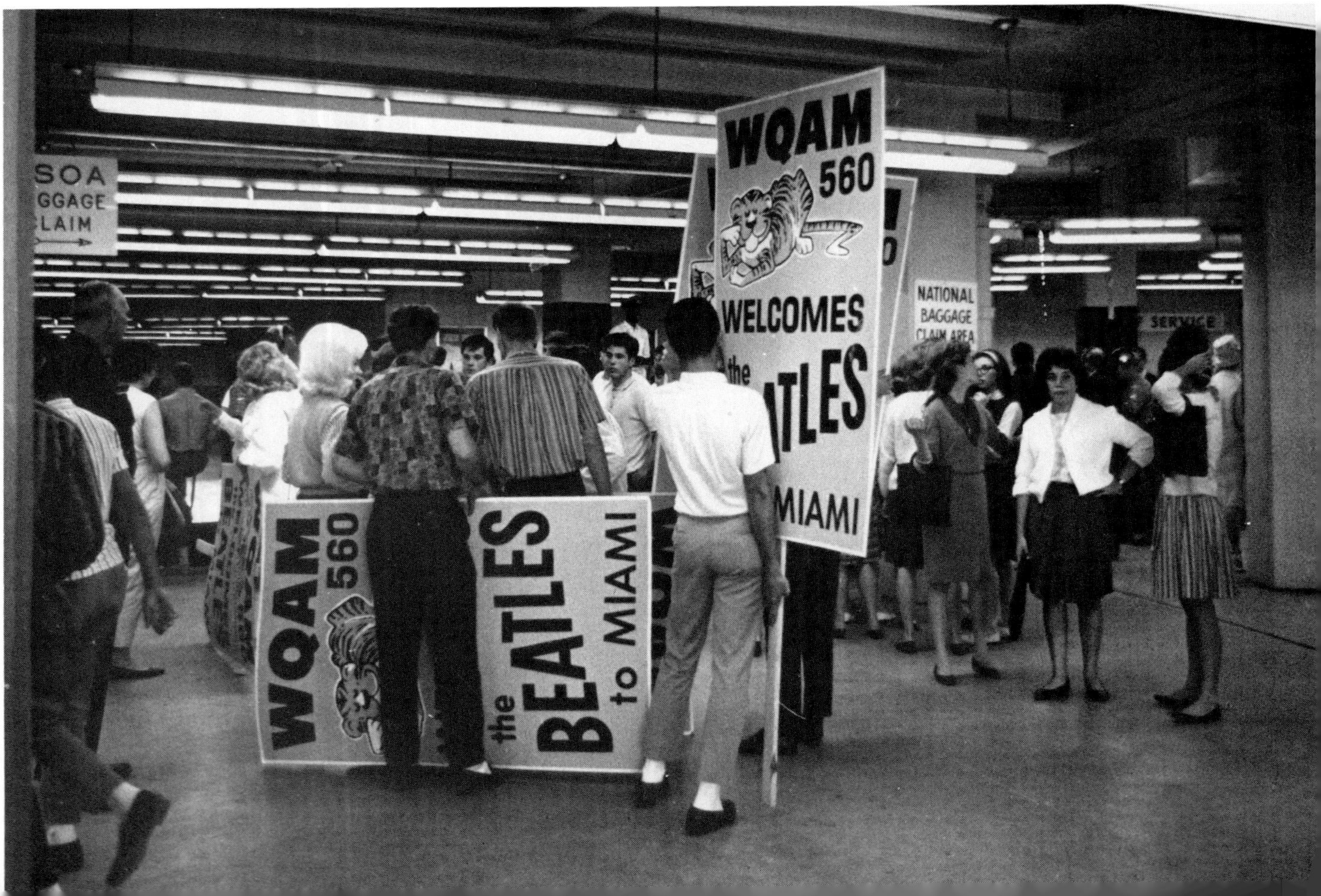
SOA
GGAGE
LAIM
WQAM
560
WELCOMES
the
ATLES
MIAMI
NATIONAL
BAGGAGE
CLAIM AREA
SERVICE
WQAM
560
the
BEATLES
to MIAMI

108

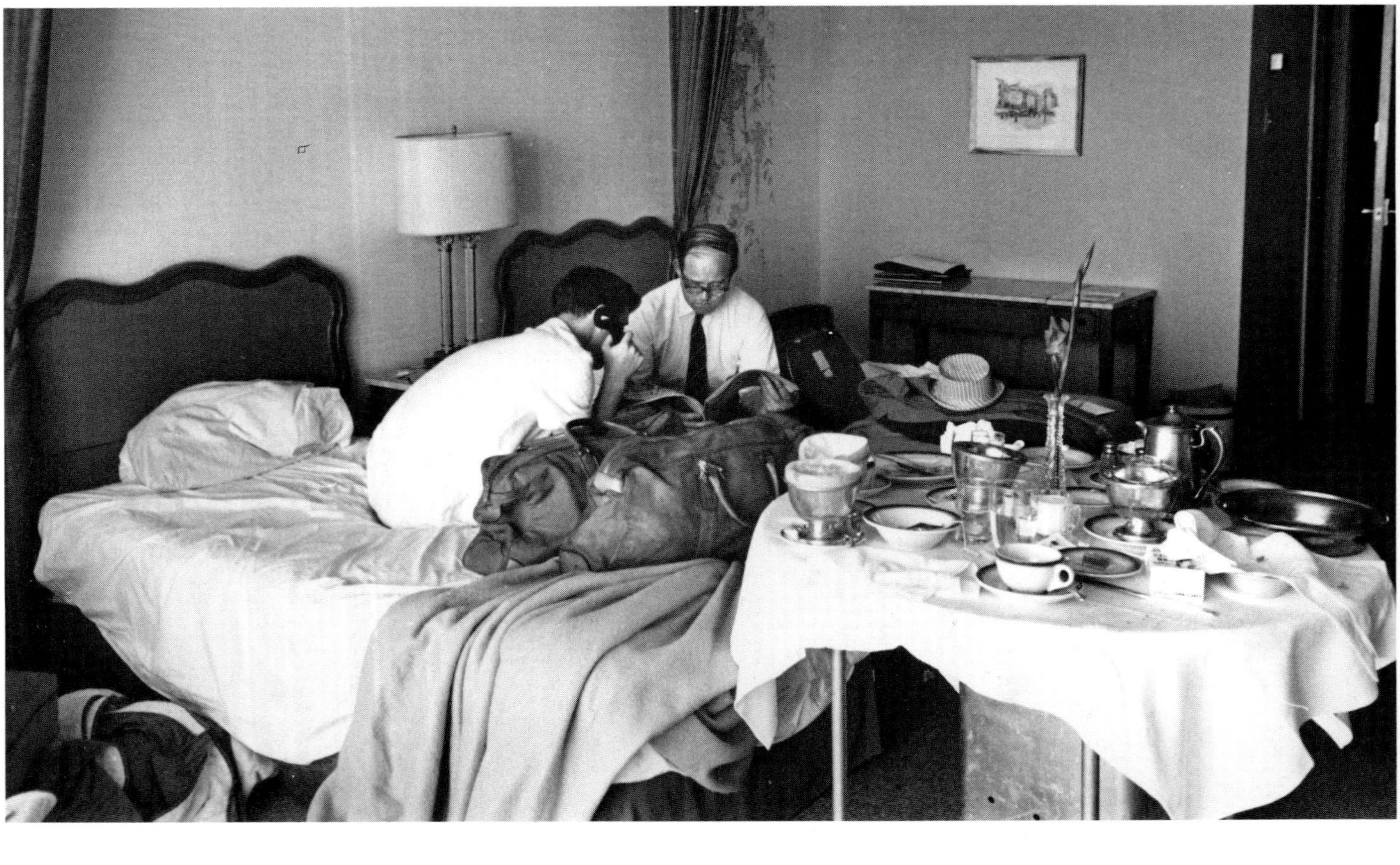

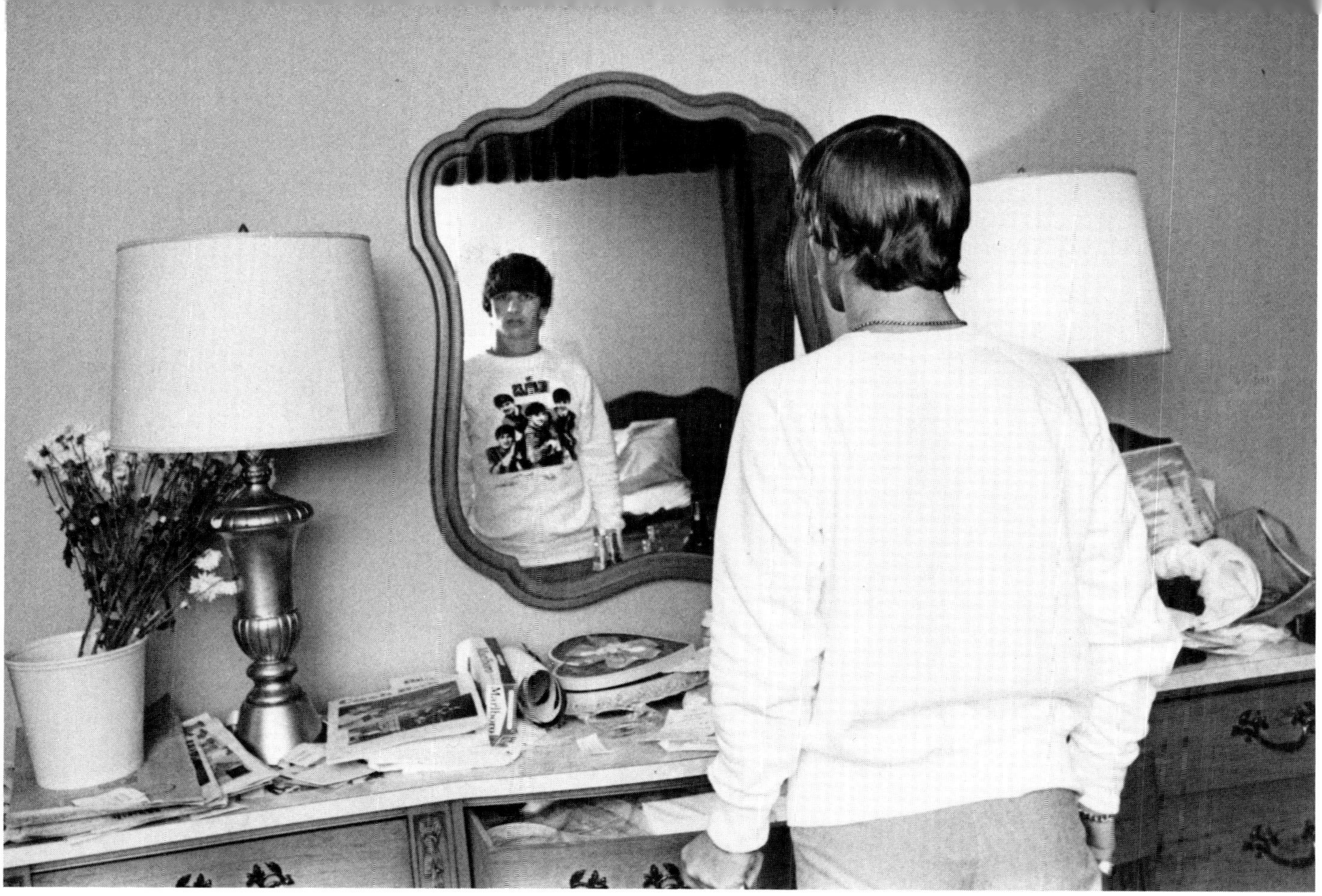

MIAMI

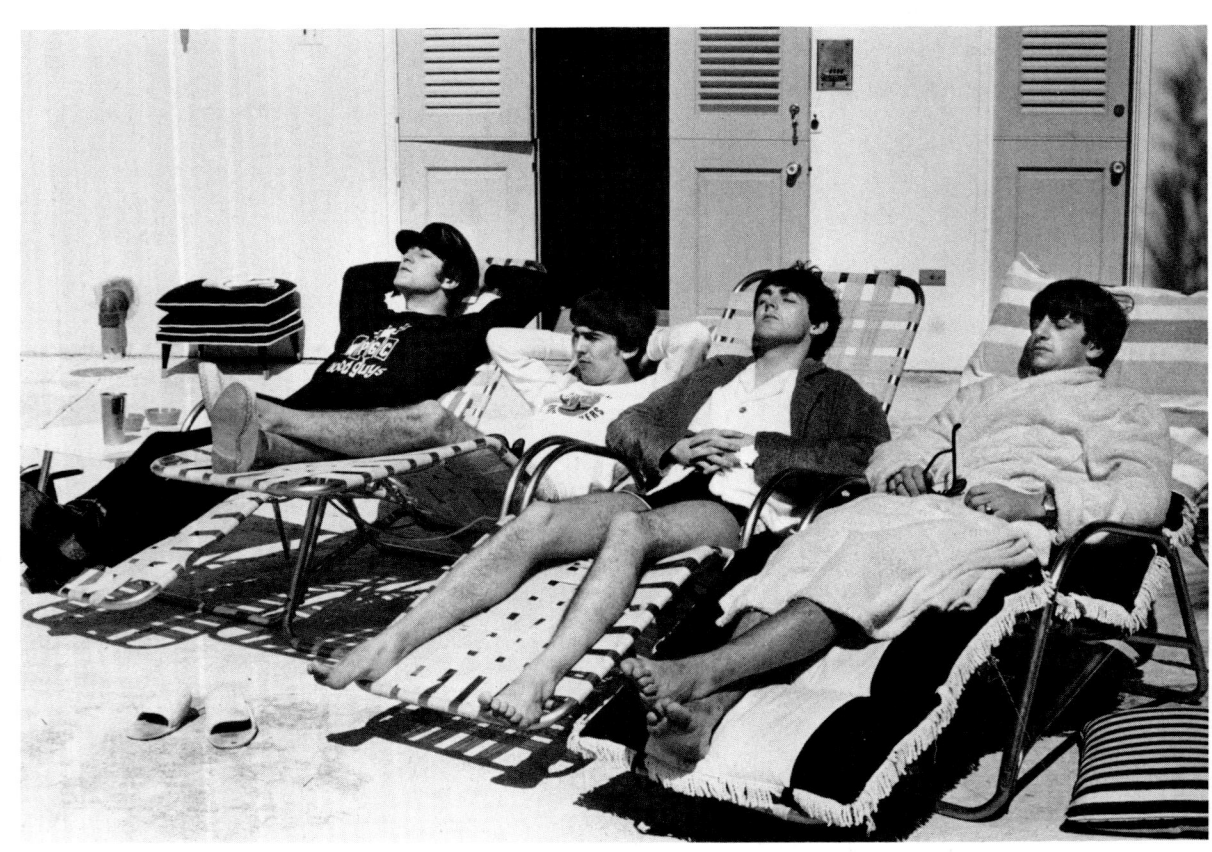

MIAMI

MIAMI

MIAMI

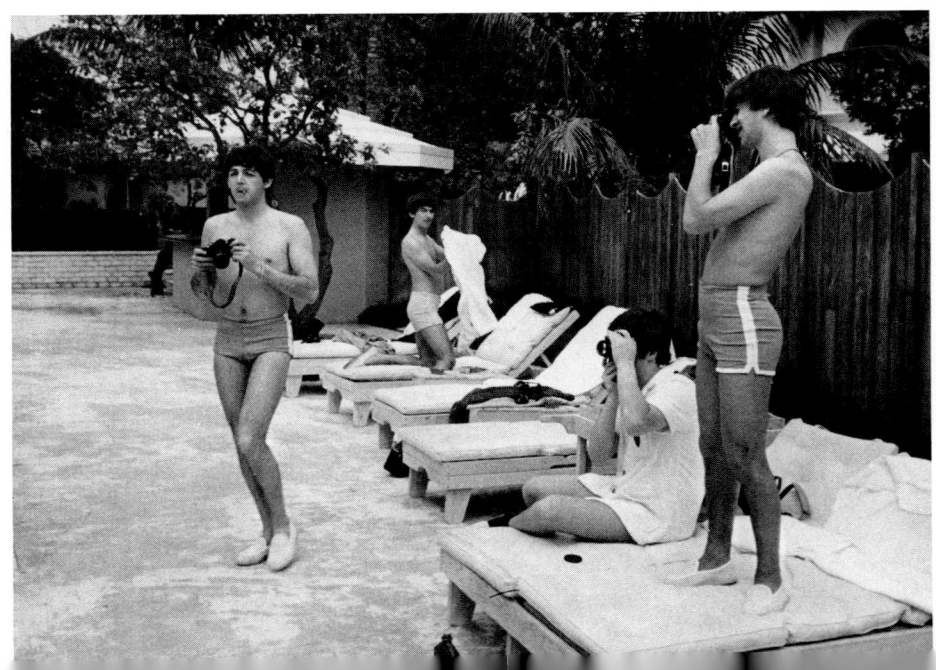

MIAMI

MIAMI

MIAMI

MIAMI

MIAMI

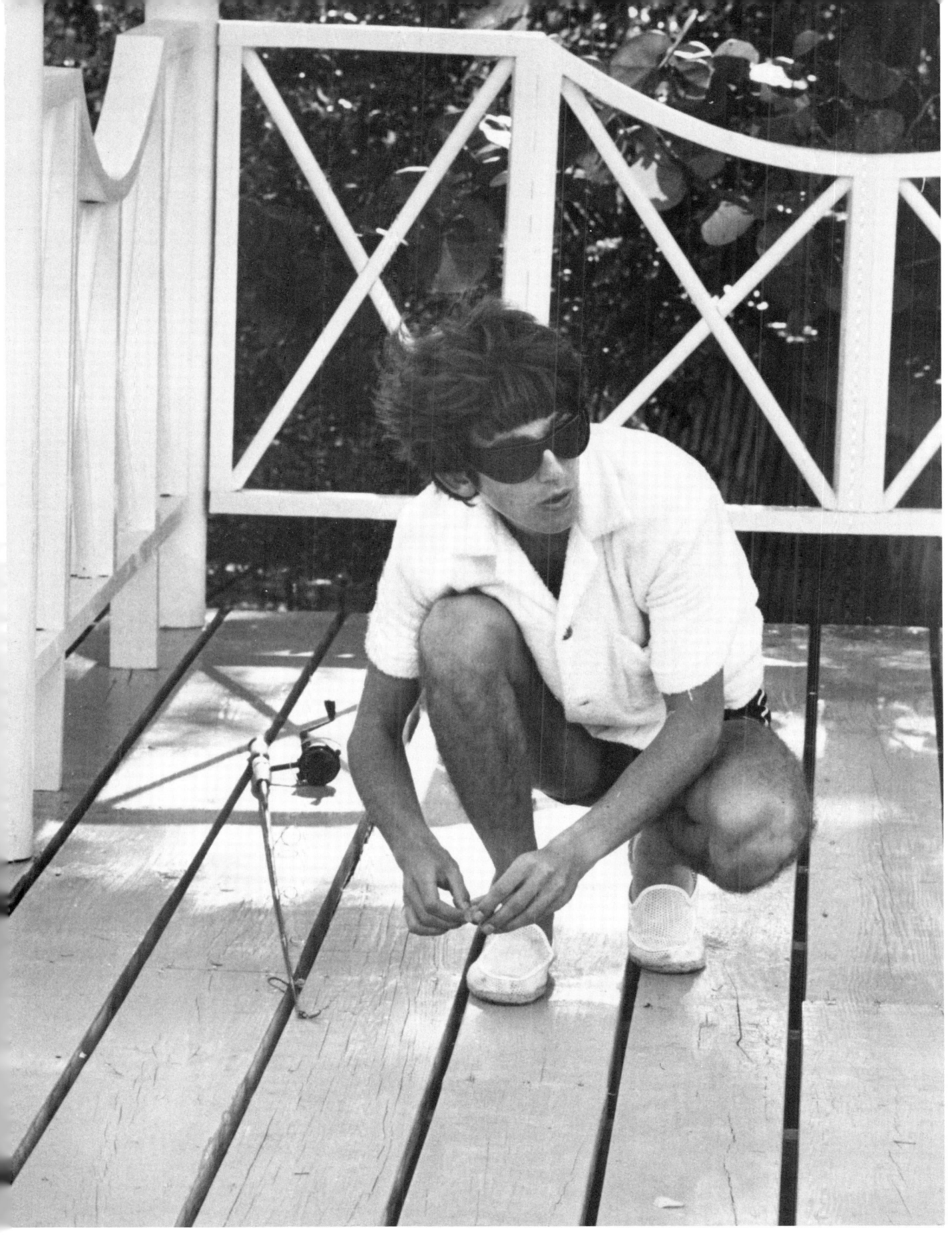

MIAMI

MIAMI

MIAMI

MIAMI

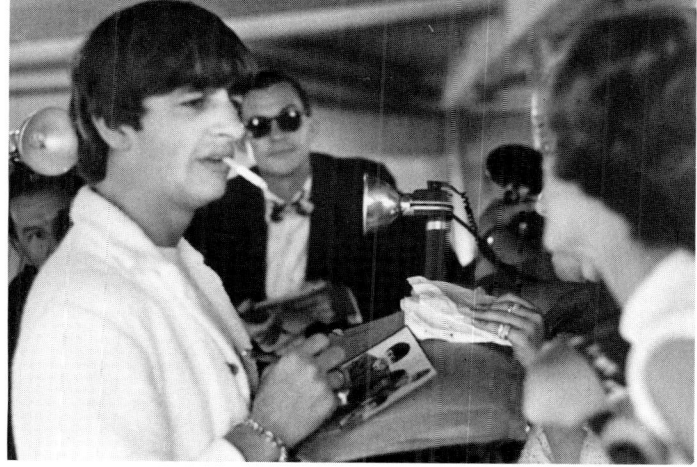

138

MIAMI

MIAMI

MIAMI

142

MIAMI

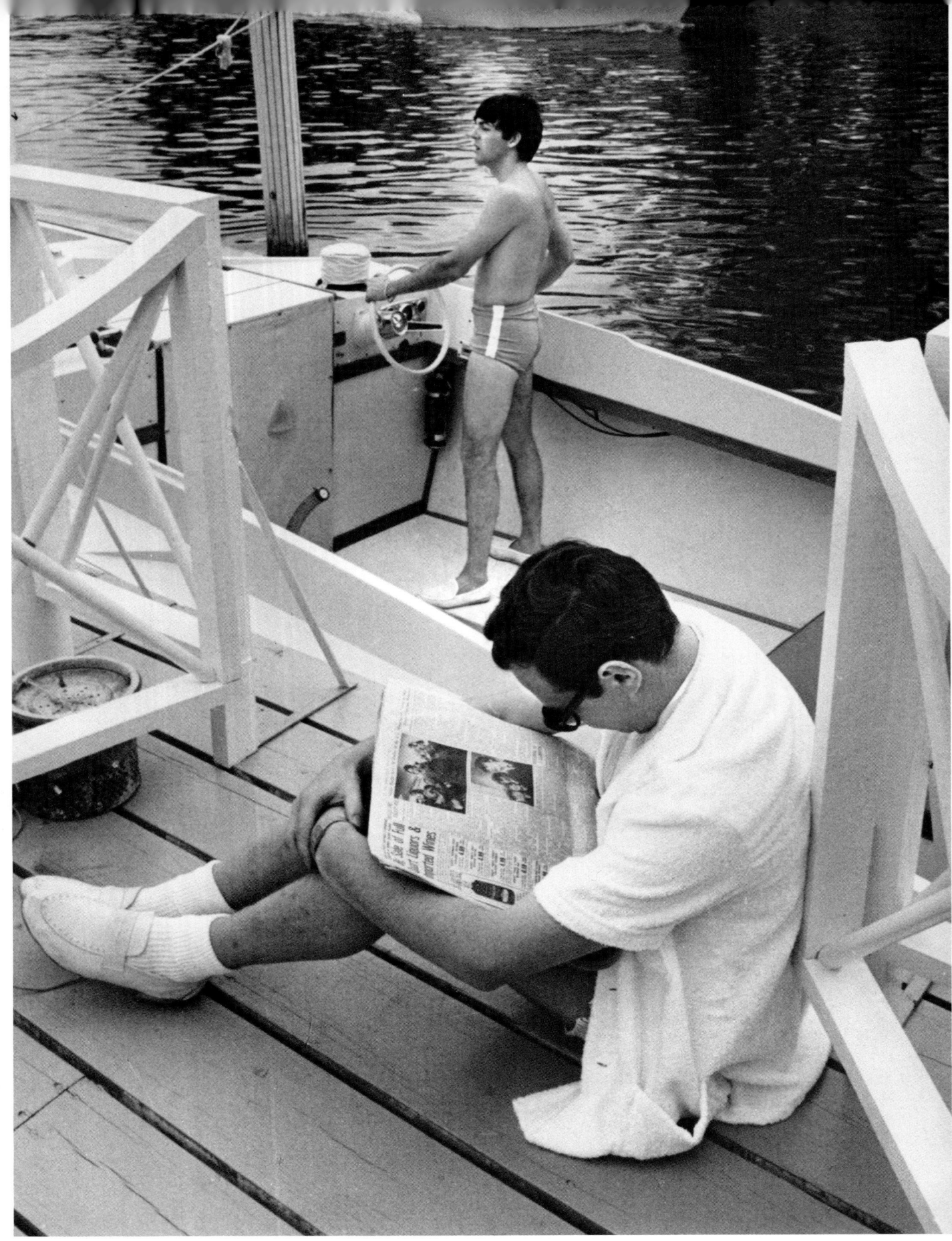

MIAMI

MIAMI

MIAMI

MIAMI

152

MIAMI

RETURN TO LONDON

For the last three days of the Miami stint, the boys relaxed on the Florida beaches, went shopping for clothes and records and caught up with the endless requests for interviews. I returned early to New York to visit some relatives, and a day or so later the Beatles flew back to Kennedy. It was time to return to London.

The Beatles' departure from Kennedy was as spectacular as their arrival. It was a night flight and the now-customary thousands of fans were there to see them off. At Kennedy airport the airplanes were boarded directly from the terminal – there was no need to go down on to the tarmac. But down there were huge crowds of kids all over the runway, climbing up the rigging at the side of the plane, even trying to get into the cabin itself. I wanted pictures of the crowds so I made my way from the lounge down to the tarmac and took some photographs of the incredible scenes.

The hardest task for the police was removing the kids from on and around the plane. If airport security hadn't had the foresight to employ so many policemen on that occasion, serious trouble could have developed. How on earth the kids were allowed to get so close to the plane I'll never know.

During the flight the Beatles tried to relax and sleep, not thinking too much about what might be waiting for them at Heathrow. Night turned to day during the flight and we landed on a Saturday morning, which was very convenient for all the London schoolkids. Special arrangements had been made at Heathrow so all three roof-level balconies of the Queens Building were open to the fans. It was truly the most fantastic welcome home imaginable, the biggest-ever greeting for the Beatles, with the loudest crowd noise they'd ever heard.

The boys were jet-lagged and weary, but the huge welcome excited them and they were full of vivid memories of the whole trip. As we came out of the plane we were confronted by an incredible number of people between the plane and the airport buildings, – mostly airport officials, airport workers, and the press. A reporter from the London *Daily Mirror* had special permission to come up from the tarmac on to the plane, and he asked me to quickly get a wide-angle shot of the Beatles disembarking against the background of the crowd and the airport buildings. It took me less than a minute to set it up; I stood at the doorway of the plane to take the picture and as the boys disembarked I asked them to look back at me. (The next day that picture filled the whole centre-spread of the *Daily Mirror*.

The sheer amount of people there caused a furore with the airport authorities because it was against regulations for so many to be on the tarmac. They held an enquiry after the incident and requested some of my pictures as evidence. I felt quite guilty because there were a few sackings as a result.

The Beatles came to America in February 1964 virtually unknown. It had taken George Martin a year to convince Capitol to release any Beatles' records, and when they finally did it was due more to pressure from DJs and the public demand than to any conviction on their part about the Beatles' prospects in the US. The DJs, the public, and George Martin were proved right; by early April the Beatles had the top five singles in all the American charts – a completely unprecedented phenomenon. Back in England they began work immediately on their first film 'A Hard Day's Night' and another American tour was set up.

The Beatles had gone to America as little more than local celebrities. By the time they returned to England two weeks later they had conquered America and were well on their way to conquering the rest of the world.

PAGES 154 & 155
Return to the Frozen North. The Beatles fly back to New York from Miami. The snow is still on the ground at Kennedy Airport. George clutches his BEA flight bag, bearing the cleverly adapted logo.

PAGE 156
The departure at Kennedy. Barriers were hastily erected to stop the frenzied fans from clambering on to the plane. It was difficult getting these pictures under such circumstances, and I had to rely on the light from car headlights and the plane itself in order to capture these crowd scenes.

PAGE 157
Top: *John is pretending to be glad to be returning to London, but in fact he would quite happily have stayed longer in the States. Eventually, of course, he made New York his home.*

PAGES 158 & 159
Luckily, there were plenty of police on hand. **Page 159, Bottom left:** *The Beatles' homecoming jet had been nicely personalised. Note the contraption for boarding the plane, which the fans swarmed over, trying to get inside the aircraft itself.* **Bottom right:** *On the flight back the boys read themselves to sleep.*

PAGE 160
Arriving to the tumultuous reception at Heathrow. **Top:** *This photo is similar to that used on the centre-spread of London's Daily Mirror the next day, except that in the Mirror picture the boys are facing the camera.*

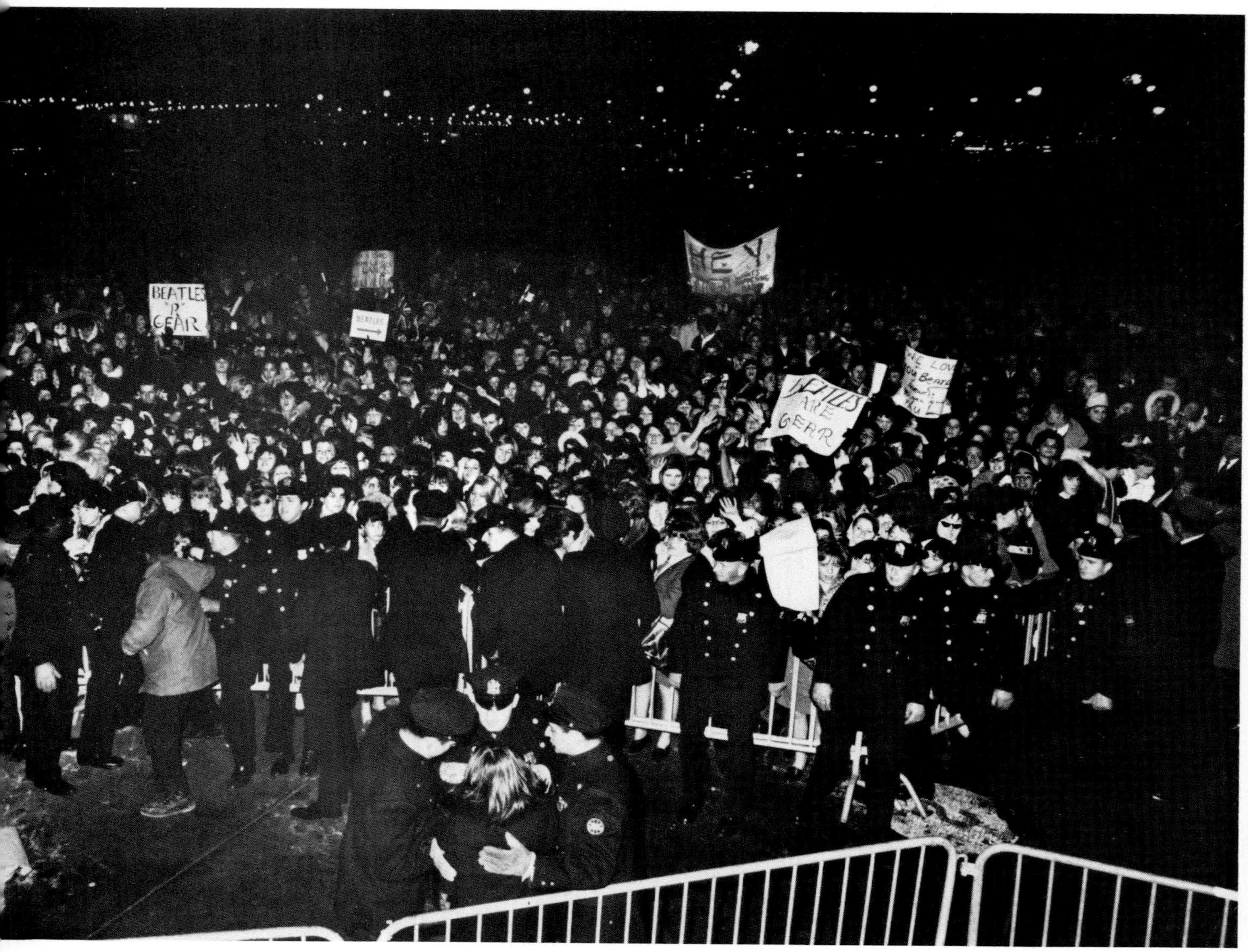

RETURN TO LONDON

RETURN TO LONDON

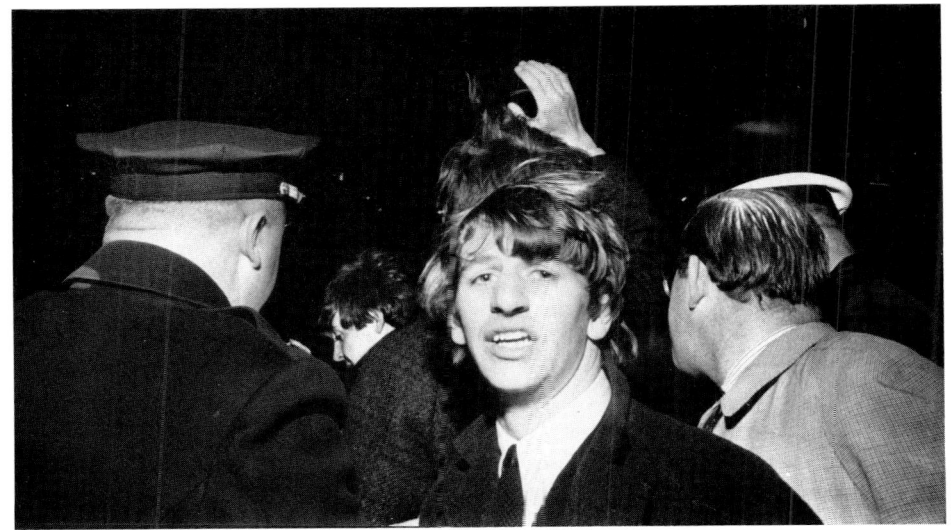

RETURN TO LONDON